DEBORAH JUNE ANNUNZIATA

WHILE WE WERE WAITING

A COMPELLING TRUE LOVE STORY OF HOPE
AND ANTICIPATION, WITH A HINT OF COMEDY

WHILE WE WERE WAITING
Copyright © 2022 by Deborah June Annunziata

All rights reserved. Neither this publication nor any part of this publication may be reproduced or transmitted in any form or by any means, electronic or mechanical, including photocopying, recording or any information storage and retrieval system, without permission in writing from the author.

Scripture quotations marked (NIV) are taken from the Holy Bible, New International Version®, NIV®. Copyright © 1973, 1978, 1984, 2011 by Biblica, Inc.™ Used by permission of Zondervan. All rights reserved worldwide. www.zondervan.com The "NIV" and "New International Version" are trademarks registered in the United States Patent and Trademark Office by Biblica, Inc.™ Scripture quotations marked (NLT) are taken from the Holy Bible, New Living Translation, copyright ©1996, 2004, 2015 by Tyndale House Foundation. Used by permission of Tyndale House Publishers, Carol Stream, Illinois 60188. All rights reserved. Scripture marked (NKJV) taken from the New King James Version®. Copyright © 1982 by Thomas Nelson. Used by permission. All rights reserved. Scripture quotations marked (AMPC) are taken from the Amplified Bible, Classic Edition. Copyright © 1954, 1858, 1962, 1964, 1965, 1987 by The Lockman Foundation.

ISBN: 978-1-4866-2347-1
eBook ISBN: 978-1-4866-2348-8

Word Alive Press
119 De Baets Street Winnipeg, MB R2J 3R9
www.wordalivepress.ca

Cataloguing in Publication information can be obtained from Library and Archives Canada.

Dedication

I dedicate this book to my dear husband, Tony, with sincere thanks for your willingness to share our personal story. I am especially grateful for your amazing sense of humour that kept our chins up, and for your untiring ability to endure and never give up. There is so much for which to be thankful and I attribute that to your ongoing strength as you referred to yourself as the "iron man." It was my privilege, as your wife, to also be your caregiver as we valiantly faced each new challenge that your health situation brought, side by side, hand in hand. Your bravery through it all was an inspiration to me and to our family. I look forward to sharing many more years together.

Acknowledgements

Tony and I would like to thank our families and our friends for all the support you have given us during this challenging time in our lives. Your love and prayers meant a great deal and saw us through each aspect of this journey.

A special thank you to our two children, Christina and her husband Jason, Steven and his wife Stacey, for being there for your parents and helping us face life together *while we were waiting*.

We want to thank my mother, June, my sister, Cheryl, and Tony's siblings Josephine, Anna and Don, Mike and Anna, and Angelo for their constant love and support throughout the whole mission.

We would like to thank our family doctor for his professional services through the years and for the constant support he and his staff gave to us as we drew closer to transplant time. Frequent visits to the emergency department at Douglas Memorial Hospital in Fort Erie were not unusual and he was always there for us. Thank you to the staff of Douglas Memorial Hospital and Greater Niagara General Hospital for the kindness and care given to Tony and the support provided for his family.

Thank you to the Hepatology Department of Toronto General Hospital for giving us hope when there seemed to be none. Your untiring guidance and counsel, as we edged closer to realizing our dreams fulfilled, gave us the comfort we needed and filled us with hope for a future together.

Thank you to the amazing transplant team who performed the miracle surgery. You made that dream come true.

Our sincere gratitude goes to the Trillium Gift of Life Network for putting Tony on the list and seeing the process through to completion, giving us a renewed chance at life together.

We are grateful to CCAC Niagara and the kind workers who came to our home to provide the care that Tony needed while waiting for the surgery. Your help meant a lot to us.

Thank you to the staff at South Niagara Life Ministries who gave of their time and counsel when we were in need of their kindness and caring hearts.

We appreciate the management and staff of the Fort Erie YMCA and Zeller's for giving me the appropriate hours and support that allowed me to keep my job and care for Tony as well.

The support and prayers of our church family at Garrison Road United Brethren Church were very important to us and meant a great deal.

We are grateful to our dear friend, Irene, for her encouragement and support of this book project, and for her untiring efforts to help with the manuscript.

Most of all, we thank God our Heavenly Father for His constant presence with us as each new facet of our journey unfolded. He listened as we prayed, cried, and in the silence when no words would come. We offer our praise and gratitude for His healing for Tony and His love that fills our lives and our home.

Foreword

Thank you my dear friends, Debbie and Tony, for giving me the privilege of being the first to read your story. Only God could have brought you through this journey with such a positive outcome. Your trust in Him along the way not only brought you strength and courage, but as you shared your faith, others also received the encouragement they needed.

I pray that God will use this book to bless all who read it and that they will know for themselves the wonderful comfort and assurance only God can give.

God bless you.
Irene Ward
Fort Erie, Ontario
September 2022

1
ACCEPTING CHANGE

In the laughter and shenanigans of family life, I often felt like I was in bliss. For many years we knew the true meaning of living the dream, a simple and nice life for us. That is, until the day we received a phone call that would change the course of our lives. The message was, "Please inform your husband that all his medical tests have come back and the doctor wants to speak to both of you about the results."

I thought about the symptoms he had been experiencing lately; fear and doubt began to course through my entire being. My shoulders slumped and instinctively; I knew this was not going to be good news. The receptionist inquired at my silence, "Are you still there?"

With hesitation, I managed to mutter, "Yes."

I tried to pilfer more information but was kindly reminded, "You have to wait to speak to the doctor."

The appointment was made for later that day. I stared at the phone for a moment trying to comprehend what just happened. With a shaky hand, I hung up the receiver. As I sat down, bewildered, I reminded myself to get a grip because my husband was going to need my strength and support.

When Tony came home from work a short time later, I told him about the phone call that his test results had come back. His expression gave him away; he appeared worried and my heart sank. It was almost time for the appointment, so no time to ponder. Very little was said on the way to the doctor's office, both of us deep in thought, trying to keep it together.

While we were waiting, we became a little silly with familiar jokes to make each other laugh as we are accustomed to doing. From the first day we met, I appreciated his sense of humor. Often during challenging times, we would bicker during our initial discomfort, then, after we wore ourselves out, we would resort to humor and accept change.

Abruptly we were interrupted when we heard his name called and were escorted to the privacy of the physician's office.

We waited silently and somewhat impatiently, as we squirmed to get comfortable. After a few pleasantries, the doctor sat down behind his desk and opened a chart. We sat side by side anxiously awaiting the results.

Sadly, the test results were not good. Tony was diagnosed with an illness for which there was no cure. Tears spilled down my face and the words finally formed, "There is hope; there has to be."

With a bit of optimism, he replied, "Absolutely." He looked at Tony and said, "Your only hope for survival would require an eventual organ transplant." This was not what either of us expected to hear.

He told us an appointment had already been made with a specialist and to pick up the requisitions for more tests on the way out. As we stood up to leave, I realized how difficult sharing this information must have been for him.

After receiving what felt like earth-shattering news, we mindlessly got in the car and drove home, speechless. I thought about the prognosis, *you may possibly have five more years until you will require a transplant unless there are complications.* I looked over at my husband wondering how he was taking the news only to see a combination of emotional pain and shock. As if he read my mind, he smiled at me to lighten the horrific moment.

My stomach had a feeling similar to plunging down the first big hill on a roller coaster. As time moved on, we remained in the comfort of denial. We continued to work, take care of our family, and keep up a somewhat normal life, until the cold reality set in as his health continued to decline. There was no stopping the hands of time as years passed by since that very grim day.

> "God grant me the serenity to accept the things I cannot change; courage to change the things I can; and wisdom to know the difference." (Reinhold Niebuhr)

2
LIFE GOES ON

While shopping for groceries for a very special occasion, my mind was miles away as I began to ponder, right beside the relish section of aisle seven, about the series of calamities we were experiencing. I thought, *how appropriate to choose this particular spot when my life appears to be in a pickle.*

Added to our already growing list of anguish, my place of employment sadly announced that it was going to close. Why I picked this moment at the grocery store to sort all this out was beyond me. I continued to think about all that was happening. Just when money was going to be tight, all the appliances began to break down, one by one, the basement flooded, and the car suddenly needed repairs. Accepting change is an understatement because there were too many things changing all at once.

On the lighter side, there was not just good news, but great news. Our daughter and son each announced they were engaged and going to get married, only two months apart! Naturally, I was elated and full of joy over both exciting announcements and delighted with the upcoming additions to our family.

Now let me clarify: that's two weddings, two 'stag and does,' two bridal showers, all within five months! And coping with an empty nest! Then there was the need to find a new place of employment and become a caregiver. The good news helped balance the sad news and paved the way to move forward with a better outlook.

While still standing in aisle seven, I was finally awakened from my reverie, when I overheard one of the employees say, dramatically, "I am having a bad day!"

I thought that statement might have been rhetorical, so, thoughtlessly, I blurted out, "We are having a bad decade!" I glanced around and noticed there were several other shoppers.

At first, they appeared to be polite, trying not to make eye contact, when, unexpectedly, everyone within earshot began to laugh, including me. My speculation was that people seemed to relate and it did sound amusing. It was interesting how laughter could be an immediate oasis for a dry soul.

With my spirits feeling a bit lighter, I topped off the conversation. "When weathering life's storms, sometimes when it rains, it pours blessings, too. Hopefully, that will be today because tonight is a very special occasion; we are celebrating our thirtieth wedding anniversary and I am shopping for ingredients to prepare a special dinner."

Everyone responded with a cheery, "Congratulations on such great news!" We exchanged a few pleasantries, and each went back to their shopping.

As I was leaving, I said to the employee, empathically, "I hope you have a better day!"

She replied with a smile, "I hope you have a better decade!"

We both expressed understanding, and then went our separate ways. Moments like this reminded me why I love our little town so much. I never mentioned our life challenges and simply enjoyed a comforting moment with the enchanting people of our community.

As I continued shopping, I thought about when we decided to settle here all those years ago. It began with Tony and me. Two years later our daughter, Christina, arrived, and two years after that our son, Steven, was born. Tony was by my side for the birth of both our children and was a great support to me. Eventually, a miniature collie named Gideon became a whimsical member of our family and brought us much joy.

As I waited my turn at the checkout, there was tenderness as I thought that even mundane things like grocery shopping, can be meaningful. I was grateful for this moment of emotional reprieve. After paying my bill, I walked to my car, filled my trunk with many grocery bags, and proceeded home.

Time was fleeting. I began to rush to unload my groceries, attempting to juggle way too many bags at once. On my way inside, an obstacle caught the handle of one of my bags and jerked my body to a complete stop. I was captured by the wrought iron railing leading up to the front porch of our house when one of the bags became entangled in the railing. The bag tore, launching boxed goods all over so I dropped the other bags that were way too heavy anyway. I was irritated.

In the past, that same railing, in my haste, would sometimes catch an article of clothing or my purse handle, and bring me to a sudden stop. This incident was always annoying, and a reminder for me to slow down. I checked to make sure that everything was okay and very thankful nothing was broken.

Feeling slightly foolish, I took a quick look around and noticed that my neighbour was watching my 'stooge' show, so I just offered a polite, "Hello." *Why do I have an audience every time I do something goofy?* But I admit, I love watching the ridiculous, too. We have friendly neighbors and they always offer a helping hand, however, this time I refused. "No worries, I've got this, and thank you for your kindness."

Trying to hide my frustration and slight humiliation, I gathered up the mess and kicked the rest of the boxed goods into the house. I waved 'so long' to the neighbour, who still seemed concerned, as he watched this 'slapstick' comedy. I gently closed the door behind me. Glaring at the grocery bags, I wished they could put themselves away because I was growing weary.

The atmosphere was very quiet and subdued, not a peep, which was unusual for a normally crazy, busy household. I checked my hubby's whereabouts, glad to see he was napping. I hoped the rest would replenish his energy and enable him to enjoy our special evening. Gideon was curled up by his feet and looked up at me with a sleepy expression. I cupped his face in my hands and I kissed his adorable face. It was a sight to behold, and my heart welled up with affection for them both.

I lingered a moment, remembering a humorous occasion during a speech at *Toastmasters*. *Toastmasters* is a course that teaches people how to speak properly in public and think quickly on their feet to answer questions. One of the students was delivering a speech on family pets when he asked, "Did you ever notice that one spouse always appears to love the dog more than the other spouse?" We all laughed at this, even though the speaker was dead serious.

When I arrived home after my class, the statement was still on my mind so, nonchalantly, I questioned *my* spouse, "Have you ever thought that I loved our Gideon more than you?"

Tony was always quick-witted, "Let me put it this way. If Gideon and I were drowning and you could only save one of us, I envision that I would be hanging on to his tail for survival as you hauled him to shore." The memory of that moment was still amusing, and I laughed as I thought about it.

After mustering up a second wind, I carefully put away the perishables, setting aside all the other ingredients meant for our special romantic, relaxing *dinner for two*. I had to remind myself to focus on the task at hand because I just nicked my finger with a dull knife. After finishing some of the preparations, I placed the food in the oven and gently closed the door.

I left the room for a moment and went downstairs to put in some laundry. As I began folding towels, I remembered our wedding vows *"To have and to hold from this day forward, for better, for worse, for richer, for poorer, in sickness and in health, to love and to cherish, till death we do part."* I quivered at the thought of *for worse, poorer, and sickness*.

With that thought in mind, I placed the towels in the laundry basket and started up the stairs. Suddenly I was startled by a loud, screeching, ear-piercing sound, one I had heard many times before!

Time had gotten away from me. In the midst of this unnecessary additional drama, I threw the basket in the air. Fortunately, most of the clean towels remained in the basket.

Immediately I went to find the cause of the noise and hopefully, soon! It was the all-too-familiar sound of our smoke alarm! As I ran up the stairs, I heard myself cuss out loud and, as always, I looked up and asked for forgiveness, while still in motion. Did I really believe that in all the almost constant state of turmoil, I could really accept change at some point? As I continued to find the cause, I gathered that in all the chaos, and the continual calamity, with an unexplainable hint of comedy, life will continue to overflow in abundance while we were waiting.

DREAMS DO COME TRUE

Even with both hands covering my ears, I could still hear the fire alarm's shrill sound when I got to the kitchen. As I opened the oven door, smoke billowed out and while waving away the smoke, I found the cause right away. Quite simply, it was just that some food had fallen to the bottom of the oven and since our trusty smoke alarm caught it early, our special dinner was not spoiled in any way.

However, the mini-drama caused my heart to beat slightly quicker than normal. As I wiped the perspiration from my brow, I thought *how remarkable that something so small could create such chaos and commotion. Better yet, it's when that one small thing turns out to be nothing at all.*

Grabbing an oven mitt, I reached into the oven, pulled out the smoldering offender, and threw it in the sink. I closed the oven door, turned on my heel, and ran in the direction of the still-blaring smoke alarm, hoping that all the commotion wouldn't interrupt Tony's nap. To add to my astonishment, he was already out of bed and flailing a giant beach towel under the alarm.

From past minor cooking situations, he had become quite an expert at this drill, and finally, the smoke alarm was quiet. Although there was a welcome silence, he continued to flail the beach towel under the alarm. I guess he was just making sure that the odd job was complete. It gave me a moment to wonder why he chose a giant beach towel instead of a face cloth or something smaller and not so awkward.

All too quickly there was another unnecessary, but familiar, sound: clang and smash! It was Tony accidentally whacking the oversized giant clumsy towel into one of my triple votive candle sets sitting safely on the shelf. Instead of just thinking it, I said out loud, with emphasis, "I should have just ordered out, there is way too much drama over one dinner." Softly I added, "I'm sorry."

Too weary to stop the flood even from the beginning, the tears streamed down my cheeks, and I began to sob out loud. As usual, Tony looked shocked; that annoyed me, and I continued to cry. With the constant chain of events, he probably thought my mini breakdown was as irritating as the alarm we just stifled. Instead of the dream of our perfect evening, it was becoming another real-life drama. I cried even more at the thought.

Discouraged and determined to compose myself, I realized I wasn't crying because of the votives breaking or the smoke alarm screeching so loudly. Sure, both were a nuisance, but I was crying because I wanted to have a perfect evening together and yet it was another '*I Love Lucy*' episode. He broke the silence and with a puzzled look, "Why are you crying?" He looked a little annoyed. I wondered *why, whenever I cried, he always looked like he was going to call 911 for backup.*

It reminded me of the day I received the call that my place of employment was closing. After I hung up the phone, I walked to the window and looked out, trying to hide my face because of the tears. When he discovered I was crying, he made a remark that made me cry even more. I became furious with him. "Whenever I cry, you always make some crass remark that is not helpful, and then you have the nerve to become angry." Raising my voice slightly, I announced, "What kind of monster are you and I don't like you very much right now."

He corrected me, "First of all, let's clear this matter up. I have never been angry when you cry. I am frustrated because I can't help you, and there is a difference between being angry and frustrated!"

My heart softened and at that moment I loved him even more than I thought possible. Still sniffling, I said, "You mean after all these years when I thought you were angry, you were just frustrated?"

"Yes, I always just wanted to help you." I smiled at the thought of what an enlightening and interesting turn of events this turned out to be.

He continued, "You know D.J., I can glue them back together!" My name is Deborah June, and he calls me D.J. as a sign of endearment. I thought to myself, *yeah, right, Super Glue.* Tony had become a superhero many times with his trusty *Super Glue*. I stopped crying, sniffled a little, and thought, *why am I starting to hiccup?* I was still determined to salvage our special day and so was he.

"I have an idea. Let's forget about this hectic moment and start afresh. Meet me in the dining room in fifteen minutes. Love yah."

He replied "Love yah, too. Everything will be alright, you'll see." He looked happy again and I felt better, too. I always loved to hear those six words *everything is going to be alright*—the perfect advice for most situations.

After all these years I still choose to see the world through rose-colored glasses. In most situations, I will opt to find a brighter side. Tony claims to be a realist and he will point out what he thinks we should know, no matter how morbid or shocking. Somewhere we meet in the middle and that's where we both share growth together in our marriage.

Thanks to my hubby's handy work with one giant beach towel the home front is safe to continue the last of the preparations for our lovely meal. I strolled back to the dining room to finish setting the table. After gathering my dishes from the buffet with an old-fashioned hutch, I threw my dusty rose tablecloth into place. Then I laid out my special Royal Dalton dinnerware which is part of the Tiverton collection. The pattern is a white background with beautiful dainty pink flowers and an ivy wreath.

I found this China to be the perfect pattern for all occasions and the dinnerware was a thoughtful gift from my mother and sister. We knew we would enjoy these dishes forever.

Next, I folded the emerald green napkins into the shell pattern. The table setting now resembled one of my favorite tea rooms I frequented. To create a romantic atmosphere, I lit my other floating, triple-candle centerpiece, with lovely flowers at the base, which complimented my ensemble. The table looked beautiful and ready for a celebration for two.

Feeling a bit lighter in heart, I smiled thinking about the nice meal we were going to share. I reached up to smooth a strand of hair only to realize there were a lot of loose strands. I went to get cleaned up, adding some fresh eye makeup and raspberry-colored lip gloss. After all these years I still felt it was important to look my best for a date with my husband even in the comforts of our own dining room. Upon taking the pins out to brush my hair, I decided to wear my hair down over my shoulders. One last glance in the mirror and I was off to put the finishing touches on our meal.

I was excited and started to run down the hallway, then down the stairs to our kitchen. On the way, I stubbed my toe on the floorboard. I sat down on the floor and shouted in pain, thinking *why must I always need a painful reminder to learn to slow down in the house, and, in life, for that matter?*

Concerned, Tony called out, "Now what is going on down there?"

My response was, "Nothing," in a really nonchalant voice. I thought *why draw more attention to yet another silly situation?*

With my toe still throbbing, I said in a cheery voice, "Dinner is ready and served in the main dining room," as I rang my dinner bell just for fun. It was a white bell with a festive background, a gift from my sister many years ago.

Tony arrived with a smile on his face, "You don't have to make all that fuss and noise. Let's eat. I've been looking forward to this meal all day. And why are you limping?" I didn't respond.

We sat down and after he said the blessing, for a brief moment we gazed into each other's eyes from across the candle-lit table. No words were spoken as we reflected on this milestone: our 30th wedding anniversary, May 28th. We were especially thankful for this precious time because, only a day earlier, Tony had been discharged from the hospital.

Before his release from the hospital, I mentioned our anniversary dinner menu to the doctor. I knew the importance of asking the specialist if he could go off his strict diet for just one dinner. We waited patiently for his answer. He said, "Since it is a special occasion (*drum roll*), yes, just one dinner and then back on the proper diet." I was thrilled, and we both thanked him. We understood how critical it was to follow his diet regulations, hoping to keep him strong enough to endure major surgery and for future good health. The doctor's answer was very important because if he said no, then it would have been no, as we were very respectful of the guidance he provided.

The menu was very important to me, not that there was any pressure over this one-time meal, but then it would be back to our regular meal program. So, I chose his favorites, surf and turf. The side dishes were steak fries for him and a baked potato with butter and sour cream for me, corn on the cob, Caesar salad, our favorite crab meat salad, dinner rolls, and butter. For dessert: cherry cheesecake and coffee. A meal to savor, prepared just the way we like it. Tony enthusiastically dug into his meal slicing off a nice mouthful of steak.

For many years I have said to my family, *"It doesn't matter what the menu is, as long as it is made with love."* This was announced especially when we were enjoying simpler meals during leaner times.

In the background the dinner music I chose was soft and romantic, a violin and harp medley of the song *"Jesus, Joy of Man's Desiring"* (Johann Sebastian Bach, 1723). This song is generally played at weddings and fancy celebrations. The music is so breathtaking that someone usually asks, *"What is the name of this song?"*

After taking another bite of my savory rib eye steak, I looked up and smiled at Tony, who, I could see, was enjoying his lobster and melted garlic butter. I was relieved to see that he had a good appetite tonight. As he smiled back, I couldn't help but notice a hint of sadness and weariness in his soft brown eyes. It was then I realized that even joyful events were exhausting to him.

Sadly, I was reminded that only two months earlier we were told, by a specialist, that Tony was going to start a series of preliminary tests, and hopefully, he would be placed on a list for an organ transplant, soon. We both silently understood there would be many challenging moments to come. For tonight, I thanked God to be sharing this celebration together in the comfort of our own home.

During dinner, I thought it was only appropriate to reminisce about our first date. *Do we dare?* That date was so disastrous I never expected a second one, or to even be sitting here talking about it thirty years later. The memory was of all those years ago when I mentioned to my college roommates that it was the most humiliating first date of all time! I also commented, disappointedly, that I was not expecting him to ever call me back.

I really liked him, and I thought he might be the one I would spend the rest of my life with, and, like all young ladies, dreamt of living happily ever after. I have always been a dreamer and sometimes dreams do come true.

"Happy Anniversary, Love!"

He smiled, "Same to you!"

"All our dreams can come true, if we have the courage to pursue them." (Walt Disney)

4
Getting To Know You

While savoring the last few morsels of our cherry cheesecake, I thought it would be fun to reminisce. "Do you recall the calamities we endured on our first date?"

Poking his fork into the cheesecake, he replied, "Yes, I do, but calamities? I thought it was a comedy."

"As I recall, in spite of my best efforts to make a sophisticated first impression, you got a sneak preview of the real cartoon character I was anyway."

"Was?" He chided, "You mean are and ever since."

I reminded him, "You have to admit there were many unusual incidences that occurred that autumn evening."

Tony appeared to have acquired a second wind after enjoying every bit of his dinner. We both lightened up and began to banter when he said, "One thing is for sure, our journey together has never been boring,"

"I totally agree, and it seems to me, that eventually, we both became part of a new series of shenanigans, while I was getting to know you. As I recall, I was nineteen years old at the time and, like some young ladies, a little nervous. My natural clumsiness and awkwardness only added to the humiliation of that catastrophic evening."

He corrected me again, "You mean comedy."

I came back with, "Speaking of comedy, what lassoed my heart all those years ago was your sense of humor."

With a hint of disappointment, "I always thought it was my good looks."

Appearing a bit winsome, "Oh yeah, that's right, it was especially your good looks."

We both started to laugh when he began to cough a little. I noticed that laughter seemed to exhaust him slightly and my heart sank. Trying not to bring any attention to my concern, I changed the subject, "Did you enjoy your dinner?"

"The best in town."

We both continued to savor each delicious bite as if it were our last meal on earth. He smiled and changed the direction of our conversation back to remind me, "As I recall, you mentioned, all those years ago, that our first date was a struggle right from when you woke up."

I thought about that morning all those years ago. Stretching and yawning and trying to awaken, I looked out the window and noticed it was a perfect fall day. It was the first week of November and the trees were at their peak of radiant beauty. The sun was shining, and the view of the city was breathtaking. At that time, during my college years, I lived in an apartment building in downtown Buffalo that housed many other students.

I thought about how autumn was my favorite time of the year, and also my mother's. It was when I tried to call her to share this moment, I discovered that my phone was broken. After a slight meltdown of defeat, I remembered that the telephone company would fix the phone free of charge. It was usually something simple like the cord needing to be replaced and I just simply had to drop it off.

The phone issue was very important. Tony hadn't mentioned the time or the place for our date, and the plan was for him to call with the particulars. So, naturally, I was disturbed, because no telephone also meant no first date. As I thought back, it was just a broken phone but at that young age, it seemed like the end of the world. I checked the clock and I had just enough time to make it to my morning class, so I would have to take the phone in for repairs later.

I had a lot on my mind that day and found it difficult to concentrate during class. While riding public transportation to get home, other passengers kept ringing the bell and that only added more to the delay. Back then there were no cell phones or other gadgets, so people usually took a cat nap, read a book, or just stared out the window and enjoyed the view of the city.

At one point the bus driver stomped on the brake a little harder than normal, sending the passengers into a forward jerk. I noticed that the people standing, slightly banged into one another, but they were all polite and apologetic. As I gathered my books that fell on the floor, I reflected that Buffalo was considered to be 'the city of good neighbours' which I appreciated. I noticed one disgruntled passenger whose lunch fell on the floor and his apple went rolling down the aisle. I wondered why I thought situations like that were funny, but only when it happened to someone else. The bus came to one last stop, and I exited.

I remembered that my friend who lived almost thirty miles away called the day before and mentioned that she would be in town tomorrow and would I like to join her for lunch? I looked at my watch and it was almost time to meet her in front of my apartment building. I really should purchase a day planner so I would stop over-filling my days. Quickly unlocking my apartment door, I grabbed the broken phone and ran back down the stairs. There she was, right on time.

Just a little out of breath, I opened the car door and climbed in on my knees, and rolled into place; she looked puzzled at the phone. "On the way, I need to drop off my telephone for repairs and then pick it up on the way back. I am waiting for an important phone call and what are the odds that the phone broke this morning? The call will be from a really nice guy, and he has already invited me for a date tonight but will call with the time and particulars before he comes. He seems really fun to be around and we laugh together. It appears that we both have a lot in common and I don't want to miss it."

She answered, as if these situations were normal, "No problem, we can drop off the phone on the way, so we won't forget it."

But there was a problem. After lunch, we picked up the phone and decided to go shopping for a few hours. We were so busy catching up that when she dropped me off, we both forgot about the phone. As I waved goodbye and watched her drive away, it dawned on me the phone was still in the back seat of her car.

Frustrated, I actually ran after her car down the busy city street, arms waving frantically, but she never saw me. I watched her drive away until I could no longer see her car. Because she lived such a distance away, I felt hopeless. Back then I was pretty hard on myself over silly mistakes, and why not start mulling over all the other thoughtless mistakes I had made, too? With my head bent low, I unlocked my front door and dragged my sorry self inside.

It was like a light bulb turned on inside my head when I got a notion there might still be hope. This was an apartment building that housed other students. I was sure someone would have an extra phone I could borrow, if only until I received this call. After banging on a few doors, someone finally answered, and I briefly explained my story. As I repeated it, I sounded like a nut, even to myself.

The young man replied, kindly, "It is okay, stuff like that happens to me all the time. Here take this phone. I have an extra and you don't have to return it until you get your phone back." He was a student about my age with dark curly hair, friendly brown eyes, and a real gentleman. His kind attitude toward my situation helped me feel better and hopeful despite my mistake.

I replied, "Thank you and excuse me. I have to plug this in *tout suite*. It's getting late."

As I started running down the hall he said, "Oh, by the way, I hope you have a nice date after all that."

When I turned to thank him, I accidentally smashed my hand into the wall as I turned the corner. He heard the bang and asked if I was alright. When I was out of his sight, I shouted back, "I'm fine," and kept running until I reached my apartment. I didn't want him to see my bright red face. *As if the story wasn't embarrassing enough, did I have to hurt my hand, too?*

Back to the moment, I mentioned to Tony, who was enjoying his coffee, "I unlocked the door and thought *no time to dwell on my inadequacies again. I have to plug this phone in,* and when I did, surprisingly, the phone rang instantly! I thought, *Wow this was meant to be!* You sounded so nice and then you invited me to a fancy restaurant, the kind you would take a date to, to be impressed. I was impressed and thrilled. I hung up the phone. I was ready, and on time."

His reply was, "I never remembered you ever being on time for anything." I have to admit that is one area that is still a work in progress.

"As I recall, you were a gentleman as you held the car door open for me while I climbed in on my knees and turned myself around. Off we went to start our first date.

"You commented, 'I have never seen anyone climb into a car like that before, knees first?'"

Naturally, I was slightly embarrassed because I was a young lady and still climbing into the car like a kid. I made a mental note to stop doing that.

"Remember the old car?"

"Yeah, my pride and joy. The midnight blue Monte Carlo." As he was daydreaming about his car, I remembered that after we exchanged a few pleasantries and drove off, how awkwardly nervous I was. My hands were a little sweaty and I kept wringing them. I looked at him for a moment and thought he was attractive and kind. I liked him and I cared what he thought of me. We approached the restaurant, and he helped me out of the car. This was a hot spot in Buffalo, and it was a Saturday night, date night, one of the busiest nights of the week.

After reading the menu, we decided to order *The Special*, New York strip steak with all the trimmings. The meal was cooked to perfection. While cutting through my steak, I nervously knocked mushrooms and sautéed onions from my plate onto the table. I looked up at him, but he didn't notice, so I quickly covered the slight mess. My side dish was a baked potato with butter and sour cream; he had steak fries, and we both enjoyed a garden salad with Thousand Island dressing. The bread was fresh-baked and comforting.

His great sense of humor was the lasso that roped me in. I love to laugh, and he appreciated that I enjoyed his sense of humor. That only encouraged more quick wit on both our parts. Abruptly, I stopped laughing and stared at my plate because something appeared to be moving. He noticed and said, "What are you looking at?"

With raised eyebrows, "It's not *what* I'm looking at. *It's what's looking at me!*"

Puzzled, "I don't get what you mean," he said.

I saw a maggot crawling out of my garnish and since I had finished my meal, I was wondering if I ate some of the critter's family members. We were both staring curiously at my plate when the waiter approached us and asked, "Is everything alright?" I remember thinking that I know people have eaten things like this before and they are not poisonous. Silently I convinced myself not to make a big deal.

I mustered up a little charm and poise. "Everything was just lovely, but please check the garnishes before serving more dishes," I pointed to the culprit. The waiter became visibly upset; knowing it wasn't his fault, I reassured him that it was okay, and that I was fine.

Tony added some lightheartedness and humour to help out with this uncomfortable situation.

In spite of our efforts, the waiter still looked flabbergasted. I chimed in, "This is our first date and I noticed almost immediately that he has a great sense of humor. I am sure that we will probably both be laughing about this for years to come. No worries."

This could have been a bigger disaster had I not remained calm and kept up the humor we were enjoying. After all the commotion ended, we enjoyed cherry cheesecake for dessert. What a perfect way to end our meal. Suddenly I got a cold chill when I thought for a moment, *Why did I add that we would be laughing about this for years to come? After all, this is only our first date. I hope I didn't sound too presumptuous and scare him away.* The thought actually scared me, too.

I smiled at him, and he didn't let on that he caught that, so I felt better and we moved on with our evening. He broke the silence and said, "I know a nice place where we could hear some good music. Would you like to go?"

"Sure!"

He got my coat and helped me slip my arms through the sleeves. I became slightly tangled up. He circled one way, and I circled the other until we met and were staring into each other's eyes. We paused for a moment when he smiled and said, "We should be going." I agreed.

After we drove off, he turned on the radio to a rock station. We had different tastes in music; he preferred rock and roll, and I liked Motown, but that was okay. We were listening to a song called, *"Stairway to Heaven"* (Led Zeppelin, 1971). I said I liked the band, the singer was Roger Daltrey, and his band was called *The Who*. He kindly corrected me and said the band was called Led Zeppelin and the lead singer was Robert Plant. Oh, well. I listened to Led Zeppelin sing the chorus, *"yes there are two paths…"*

I thought *the new path I am on tonight with my new friend is great and he is a pleasant change to the road I have been on. I am glad we met.* The drive to the little bistro didn't take long. It was crazy busy everywhere as the evening hours approached on a classic Saturday night in Buffalo. Cars were parked everywhere. At just the right time, a car pulled out leaving a spot for us. How nice. I decided to stop thinking about all the awkward situations and stop being so hard on myself, determined to salvage our first date.

We entered the bistro. It was charming; white tablecloths and candlelight adorned each table. It was very quiet with soft music playing in the background. He held the chair out for me to sit down and joined me across the table, eye to eye. I felt a bit cornered and rather awkward. *And when did it get so warm?* He ordered a beer for himself and a glass of wine for me, and we started to laugh about some of the earlier mishaps. I began to feel a little more comfortable, so I shared with him about the earlier telephone escapade. He didn't laugh at the silliness; instead, he looked annoyed that I had to go to so much trouble. The conversation was delightful. "I like the way the candlelight makes your eyes sparkle." I started to blush and changed the subject so the heat in my face would fade.

A welcome intrusion—the waiter approached us. "We are going to become very busy soon. Is it alright if I push your table back to clear space for the dance floor?"

We both said, "Sure," at the same time, and helped him slide the table over.

Time flew by and I noticed that all the tables surrounding the dance floor became filled with many glasses, some half empty and some still full. Young men and ladies would just drop their unfinished drinks on any table available and proceed to the dance floor with their partners, all having a good time. Our table had many of their glasses, too. At that time, I was shy about saying I needed to take a trip to the ladies' room, but I excused myself as lady-like as possible. As I stood up, more mortification came; the tablecloth and I somehow became entangled and I pulled it along with me, accidentally spilling all the drinks on my date, and perhaps for the last time. I looked back and he was flailing his arms to stop the unexpected flood. I was humiliated. I didn't even stop to help him, but cowardly ran all the way to the ladies' room not even stopping to look back.

After closing the door, I stood for a moment staring in the mirror and said, out loud to my reflection, "What is wrong with you?" Once again, I was being hard on the poor soul staring back at me. I could hide in the ladies' room for the rest of the night until he got the hint and left. After all, at this point, I was sure he would never call me again anyway. So, with that thought, I started to gain some courage and strode back to the table. To my surprise, he was glad to see me and never mentioned the incident, and neither did I.

It was getting late as he drove me back to my apartment. I didn't invite him in because I figured this was not only our first date but probably, from the series of events, our last. We said our goodbyes. He reached out and gave me a tender kiss. Our first kiss. It was so nice.

Tony took a sip of his coffee, and kind of slurpy, too, when I was brought back to reality. I guess, after all these years, he had become very comfortable with me. "By the way, the part about when you plugged in the phone and you thought it was miraculous that it rang right away, I had called many times before you picked up."

"Really, for over thirty years, I thought you just called at that particular moment, and it was a sign we were meant to be."

With raised eyebrows, "Now you are telling me that the whole thing was a farce!" We both started to laugh, and I could see he was becoming very fatigued.

Gently I said, "Why don't you go upstairs and watch your TV show while I clean up?"

He agreed, "Good idea, but come join me for a while first."

We climbed into our cozy bed and started to cuddle when he said, "As I recall that story had a happy ending. I called you the next day and asked if you would like me to drive you the long distance to get your telephone back."

"I remember that was your way of inviting me out on a second date, and we had lunch and dinner together that Sunday".

He said, "I enjoyed our crazy first date, and I knew from the start that I would call you the next day and forever after. It was love at first sight."

I smiled, "Me too," as I watched him drift off to sleep. We both seemed to have fallen into an even deeper level of love, and our anniversary party for two was a success.

5

FLASHING RED LIGHT

As we know, a flashing red light indicates the need to make a complete stop, and a flashing yellow light means to proceed with caution. If only these flashing lights could be a reminder to parents to make a complete stop or use caution when teaching children as they grow into adulthood, knowing when it is time to speak, time to use caution, and especially when to make a complete stop with the lectures. A green light would be handy now and then as they grow up enough to make their own decisions, we would willfully mind our own business.

Along with the continuing preliminary medical tests and many appointments, I realized there would be no breaks from other life lessons or events. There were many times I wanted to put everything on hold until we had answers to our future, but the green light of life continued to move us forward. As I mentioned earlier, our two grown kids would be getting married two months apart, and even with all the unknown personal concerns for my husband, there was still a tender side of me that was so excited about the weddings that I could burst. My heart was spilling over with joy that my children had met their future partners to share their lives with, and I was hoping that Tony's health would hold out, so he could walk our daughter down the aisle. My eyes were tearing just thinking about it.

It was time to accept yet another big change, the empty nest. With our children soon to be moving out, I needed to understand the old quote *"time to cut the apron strings"* which I probably should have accomplished long ago. I could still recall my mother lecturing me during my college years. I remember reciting that expression to her, just to make a point, reminding her that I was a grown-up, and it was time for her to *cut the apron strings*. After saying that, I noticed my mother appeared to be dejectedly hurt by this.

I didn't understand why she looked that way at the time, and I felt no remorse. Time has moved forward very quickly, and I am now in her shoes, the shoes of a mother with grown children. I didn't see it coming, and there it was, dangling in my face, the old expression *cut the apron strings*. I remember thinking, *what knucklehead thought up an expression like that anyway?* So, I decided to Google the expression and to my surprise, there was no name attached to it. Sadly, I had to admit, reluctantly, whoever said that was right.

Today was a very special day set aside for my daughter, Christina, to introduce me to her in-laws-to-be, Jay's parents, the folks with whom we would eventually be sharing grandchildren, birthdays, and holidays.

When Tony and I met Jason for the first time, we both thought he would be a wonderful match for our daughter and a great addition to our family. Christina had already been acquainted with Jay's parents and I became pleasantly lost as I recalled the day when I met *my* in-laws-to-be for the first time. I remembered comparing that meeting to the stress of a job interview. Because I cared what they thought, it was important to me to put my 'best foot forward' and, hopefully, make a good first impression. I felt the same today about meeting Jay's parents for the first time.

Christina had volunteered to do the driving. So, there was no discussion over who was going to drive this evening because I love being chauffeured. We chatted about where we were going to have dinner—one of our favorite subjects is food. Like most people, we are a very 'foodie' family. To have more time to shop, we decided to have our dinner at the food court at the mall after meeting Jay's parents. She suggested a Mediterranean dish called *Shawarma* which I had never tried before. I agreed it would be fun to try something different.

After about a half-hour drive, we approached Jay's house and were warmly greeted by his parents. I realized we were blessed because, immediately, I felt comfortable in their presence. I glanced at Christina and noticed that she appeared happy and comfortable. Early into the visit, I could clearly see our son-in-law-to-be was a 'chip off the old block'. His mom and dad were delightful and very hospitable. Instantly I felt a family kinship with Bruce and Lori and began to look forward to sharing grandchildren, birthdays, and holidays with his folks. Of course, the mind loves to indulge in pleasant thoughts of future grandchildren. The first step though, the wedding. After a lovely visit, we said our *so longs* and waved goodbye.

Next on the agenda was a fun evening of shopping at the nearby mall and a relaxing dinner together. However, there was one more event that *I* had planned. I had a hidden agenda of my own. After our nice dinner, I was going to discuss my daughter's driving skills with her, or lack thereof. At this point, I naively believed my lecture would be helpful, and maybe it could be considered a yellow flashing light of caution. I had a speech all prepared in my mind, and we all know even the best-laid plans can go astray. It never occurred to me that, instead of a lecture, it might be time to move forward with a 'green light,' and now might be as good a time as any to *cut the apron strings.*

For a moment I let the thought go, started to relax, and enjoyed the scenery. We were driving through the heart of beautiful Niagara on the Lake when I began to recite in my head what I was going to say, diplomatically, so I wouldn't ruin an already perfect evening with one of my lectures. Suddenly there was a flashing red light, followed by a loud siren. "Are we being pulled over?"

Christina looked at me sadly, and confessed, "I just got a speeding ticket a month ago." My heart sank for her. No longer caring about my lecture, at this moment I just want to protect her from life's situations. She wasted no time and pulled over immediately. To my mortification, she was obviously used to the drill. When the officer approached the car, instead of minding my own business, I felt the need to control the situation out of love for my little girl, who I had to remember was now a young lady. Besides, I was reminded there is a fine line between caring and controlling.

I panicked and said, "This is my fault officer, I'm not feeling very well."

Annoyed, he leaned into the car to make direct eye contact with me, and said, very seriously with a very disturbed look, "Did you instruct your daughter to step on it?" Christina and the policeman were both staring at me, neither the least bit amused, waiting for an answer. I said nothing and sank into my seat, thinking I should have stayed out of this mess. I was disgusted with myself that I reacted so foolishly. I thought, *how embarrassing, and to think I prayed over all of this before we even left the house.*

And there it was, the taste of humble pie, a great big slice and not so delicious either. The humiliating red-in-the-face expression was answer enough and I said nothing. The officer directed his attention back to my daughter and said, "Do you have any previous driving records?"

She answered politely, "Yes officer, I do." I was proud of her honesty. He went back to his car for quite a while. I guess this was the time we were supposed to reflect, and we did, very quietly. Finally, he came back, and he was very kind. He did give her a ticket because of her previous record, but he lowered the charges. She thanked him and off we went. While we were trying to get back to our evening of shopping and dinner, she appeared so unsettled. I felt her pain. Obviously, there was no need for a lecture, just understanding, and love.

We made it to the mall, and while enjoying our dinner, I confessed, "By the way, I have had my own share of speeding tickets." Not my finer moment, but I felt it necessary to share this with her. She smiled at me. It was then I realized not every situation requires a lecture or discipline. My prayer was answered, in God's own way, not mine. We enjoyed a special moment together and the *Shawarma* Mediterranean food she introduced me to was scrumptious. After a fun time shopping, we went home and never mentioned the incident again.

The next morning after everyone left, I was enjoying a quiet moment thinking about all that had happened the evening before, especially the part about *cutting the apron strings*, when abruptly, the phone rang and startled me. I answered it, and to my surprise, it was my mother. I thought, *what are the odds of her calling at the exact moment I wanted to tell her all that happened?* Instead of asking her how she was, I immediately went into the story. When I told her the part about *cutting the apron strings,* I could still hear the sadness in her voice as if it were yesterday all over again. *Wow, this is a timeless emotion for mothers.*

After feeling her pain, I thought it was necessary to apologize, and then I told her, "I understand."

She said, "Why are you thinking about that now? Did something happen?" How intuitive.

Then I answered, "Well, yes, something did happen," adding, "and I had a great big slice of humble pie, too."

She said, "Go on." My mother was all ears. She was always a great listener. I rehashed the humble pie story. She was very understanding, and we both found it humorous. Harry S. Truman made this famous quote about his mother: *"No one in the world can take the place of your mother. Right or wrong, from her viewpoint you are always right. She may scold you for the little things, but never for the big ones."*

Later that day as I shared this story with my friend, Irene, I felt humiliated all over again. To my surprise, no lecture from my friend, either. She just laughed in her heartfelt way and said, "Debbie, you were just naturally protecting your young." We laughed and she added something beautiful, "Always remember, a mother will always be a mother."

Be Yourself

The mere thought that our local, dearly loved store, our work home, would soon be closing became overwhelming. That all-too-familiar gnawing in the pit of my stomach reminded me it was crucial to find a new place to work. Every area of my life seemed disturbed or disrupted nowadays. The important part was actually finding the time to hit the pavement while currently still working and keeping up with Tony's many appointments. Although distressed, I understood time would not stand still while waiting for pending medical test results with the hope of a transplant to save his life. The fact was there would be many other challenges to face *while we are waiting*.

Readjusting my thoughts, I began to dream that, after twenty-eight years of employment with the same company, there just might be another place to work. The thought was enchanting. What's more, as Tony's health continued to deteriorate, it was only a matter of time before he would have to stop working, too. That fact caused him more grief, and quite often he would worry about our finances. I didn't want to add more misery to his uncertainties with my predicament. My objective was to find a new place to work and soon, so there is one less area of our lives with a need for concern.

One day, while dropping off donations at our local counselling centre, I mentioned to one of the directors it was time to become proactive and start looking for a new place of employment. I asked, "Since you have so much experience with interviewing people, do you have any pointers?"

"Just be yourself!" was her advice, simple and nice.

At the time I had been a volunteer for many years at South Niagara Life Centre (now South Niagara Life Ministries). Since I had a long-time relationship with the staff, I trusted her advice. On the drive home, while contemplating the many changes in my life, for a brief moment I wondered, *who is 'myself?'*

I began to reflect on the actual day I received yet another life-changing phone call. The day our store manager called, I already knew what the outcome was going to be just as I said, "Hello." Several of our franchises had already closed. Being on the *'chopping block'* was not pleasant, and I was informed we were next. The part I remember most about that call was the caring way the manager told me, trying to soften the blow. She explained that in the process of liquidation, we would still have a job for approximately another year. I thanked her for calling and understood that this was not easy for her, given the fact she too was losing her job.

Tony sat quietly across from me, taking in the whole conversation. I said out loud, for confirmation, "I am losing my job and up to this point I have never been out of work." I rose, walked to the window, and looked out with my back to him, trying to hide the flow of tears.

Then he asked, "Are you crying?"

I took offense at his tone. Then I began to sob out loud, no longer sad, but very annoyed that he was onto me. "After all these years you should be able to be delicate with me when these situations arise?" With additional irritation, "Why is it that when I'm reduced to tears, you always appear angry?"

He questioned, "Angry? I have never been angry when you cry, not now, and never in the past! I am frustrated because I want to help you and, in some situations, my hands are tied. That is what frustrates me!"

Shocked by this important revelation, I stopped sobbing, and to make sure we were on the same page, "You mean after all these years you were not angry, and you just wanted to help?"

"Yes."

I thought *why is it that his emotions always appear angry?* It never occurred to me that he was frustrated and wanted to help. I thought he was disappointed with me, and this must be some kind of failure on my part. Unexpectedly, I was concerned about what Tony, and I had just learned as a couple, after this misunderstanding, and realized it was possible to move to yet a deeper level of love. "I love you, Tony"

"I love you, too. Don't worry, everything will be alright." My favorite inspiring words!

Soon the sensation of shock was over. It was time to hit the pavement and begin to seriously hunt for work while keeping in mind I must stay at my present employment to the end of liquidation to receive the grand prize–severance pay. That extra money would come in handy with our two children soon to be getting married. A new job to help out financially was a necessity, and at the same time, I would need to be totally available to care for Tony's health and future. My strength and support for him took precedence in this heap of uncertainties.

With all that in mind, I called our local Job Gym. The receptionist was encouraging and made an appointment for me right away so we could get started. Although nothing had changed, I felt a ray of hope. I was convinced there would be a new job for me! After looking over the courses that were offered, including help with my resume, and even a course to help with confidence during job interview stress, I felt I was prepared. Once again, they reminded us to, *"Be yourself."* I was grateful that our town offered programs to help get us back on our feet.

As it was my day off, I thought a morning swim at our local YMCA might help to relax my worrisome thoughts. The heated pool gave me a sense that I was on a holiday, and for a moment it provided a retreat from my troubles. I appreciated this pool. At some point, I began to pray very deeply and I mentioned to God exactly what I was looking for in the hopes of a new job. Most important in that prayer, I asked for a job that would enable me to take care of Tony first and foremost.

As I prayed, there was a gentle whisper and a spiritual tap on my shoulder to look up. I had a clear view of the front desk, and I became motivated to ask for work. With hope, I hurried out of the pool, dressed quickly, and mustered up some courage to ask if they were hiring. The nice lady who responded was the supervisor. I had only a brief moment to sell my skills and *'be myself.'* When I finished, she encouraged me to bring in my resume. She was delightful and I imagined what a blessing it would be if she became my new supervisor. Right behind her was a wall with three panes of glass and in big print were the words *body, mind, and spirit*. It was inspiring, and there was an overpowering sense that I belonged there.

With enthusiasm, I drove home, and once again the wrought iron railing stopped me in my tracks. Slightly annoyed, I carefully untangled my gym bag handle from the culprit that has been an obstacle for years. In the past, when that occurred, instead of learning to slow down, it would only irritate me. Now I appreciated the necessary reminder to slow down. As I was beginning to age, reality was setting in. *I need to take these cement steps a little more seriously.* Also, when exiting the car in a rush, I had caught my foot in the door more times than I cared to admit. Often, Tony has to remind me to wait for the car to come to a complete stop before barrelling out the door. A slow roll and hopping out were not options anymore.

I continued my attempt to get through the front door carefully so there would be no more delays. With excitement and enthusiasm, I hollered, "Tony, where are you?" He spoke in a muffled, yet familiar, voice, and then appeared with his toothbrush sloshing in his mouth. Slightly disappointed, I said, "When you are finished brushing your teeth, I have news." *Why is it that every time I have important news to share, the person I want to share it with is never available right away?* I waited eagerly. When he finally came into view, it seemed to me he would have been quicker if he were walking backward. He appeared to be in no hurry, while I am bursting at the seams with big news, and that annoyed me!

As we reclined in our usual comfy wingback chairs, I began to share with him everything in the quick version without too many details. I learned through the years that he liked for me to get right to the point. When I finished my story, he began to speak.

To my surprise and disappointment, he nonchalantly announced, "I am going to fix the cupboard door in the kitchen you have been complaining about."

Annoyed with his lack of interest, I repeated, "Complaining? Didn't you hear a word I said?"

"I heard. That is all great, but you still didn't get the job yet."

I cringed. I couldn't feel more discouraged at this moment. I cared deeply about what my husband thought, and his lack of enthusiasm crushed me.

Feeling the need to get him back on the 'same page' with me, I said, "I know that, but there is a powerful ray of hope." I continued the uphill battle of communicating with my husband, the realist. "You know, Tony, it is just like the story about the new sprout in the midst of the dead tree stump. My job is basically dying a slow death and now there is hope of a new sprout of a job that I would love."

"Well, I will get excited when you actually get the job." My joy dropped another notch, and I have to admit that sometimes I do 'jump the gun.' In an effort to save the day, he understood my need for positive feedback, "Sounds like you have a good chance of getting the job!"

We both left the room to get ready for the day. When I went upstairs to change from my gym clothes, I looked in the mirror and saw disheveled scraggly-haired, runny eye makeup, and a bewildered expression staring back at me. I thought to myself, *what a mess!* Then reality kicked in, and I shouted, "OH NO"!

Tony said, whimsically, "What now, crazy lady?" I ignored the last part of his statement.

"Come look at me. I'm a mess!"

With a puzzled expression, he said, "So?"

I gave him a nudge. "I just asked someone to hire me, and this is what I looked like when I asked her."

He started to laugh! "What is so funny? You are too much, always making a big deal over nothing."

I quizzed him, "Really, you think it is nothing?"

"Isn't that a place where people work out and they are supposed to look messy? I am sure she thought nothing of it."

I felt relief. "I guess you are right."

It sank in, no big deal. Through the many years we shared together I noticed that when we finally came to an understanding, he had a knack for making me feel better. He had developed the important skill of bringing me 'back to the planet.'

While still enjoying the day off, I finished my chores, then cleaned up, and made myself presentable. Our lunch was simple and nice, a tuna fish sandwich, with a medley of fruits and vegetables on the side for us to share. Amid the many demands of life, it was a pleasure that we could totally enjoy a nice day right here in our own home. After lunch, we grabbed books to read, crawled into bed, and prepared for a nice nap. Although I never took naps in the past, I would still wander upstairs and encourage Tony to rest as the doctors recommended. I made it more of a natural thing to do rather than make an issue out of it. Eventually, the nap became a very important part of my health and well-being as well.

Sometimes we would turn on the TV and watch westerns—*Gun Smoke, Bonanza,* or *Rifleman.* We enjoyed our time together even in the mundane things. Before we drifted off, I asked Tony, "Do you think I will get the job?"

He replied, "I know you'll get the job!"

I smiled and kissed him as we embraced, so cozy, until he fell fast asleep.

Time got away from us, and eventually, I found myself on my way to the interview. It was only natural to feel a bit jittery. My goal was to find a new job before my other job came to an end, with the hope this transition would be smooth rather than painful. The position I was being interviewed for seemed like a great fit, and what made it perfect was that it is close to home. After parking, I didn't just jump out of the car eagerly. I took a brief moment to take a deep breath and calm the butterflies in my stomach. I reflected on the advice from the director at the centre to *'be yourself.'*

While still sitting in the parking lot mustering up the necessary courage, I recalled one day while taking out the garbage, my neighbor from across the street asked how we were doing. I knew to give him an update on Tony's current health condition first. After sharing the particulars, I mentioned I had a job interview coming up, and the common discomfort I, and most people, experience during the anticipation of it. He mentioned an award-winning idea: combat breathing. This technique is used to calm men in combat. I reminded my unleashed nerves that compared to a battle, this was only a job interview. So, to relieve the stress, I took his advice and slowly inhaled for about four seconds, held it for a few seconds, then slowly exhaled, and repeated it. Then I prayed, *"If this is the job for me, please put the right words in my mouth and help me to be calm in this very stressful situation. Thanks for all the ongoing support."*

The interview began with two ladies hosting it. They introduced themselves as Sharon, the manager, and the other nice lady smiling at me was Danielle, the membership director. At first, I felt a little outnumbered but soon noticed they were kind and appeared to be rooting for me. I felt very comfortable and at ease, answering their questions as best I could. After the interview was over and we parted ways, I got back in my car and took a deep breath, so glad it was over. I looked in the review mirror and noticed the red blotches on my neck. I wore a turtleneck because I knew when I was nervous, my neck got blotchy, but they spilled over for everyone to see anyway. I wished they weren't so noticeable because I knew they saw them, too. As I drove home, I began to second-guess a few of my answers. Remembering that I prayed for the right words, I needed to stop overthinking, and I thanked God for the opportunity.

A whole week went by and I hadn't heard from them. Anyone who has ever been for an interview knows every day that goes by becomes more intense. I reminded myself it was only my first interview. The very thing we were not supposed to do was call, but, I did, and the nice lady said what was already obvious. Naturally, I was trying not to feel defeated and thought of this as practice for the next interview. I began to mull over the interview and all I could remember was: *be yourself,* and yet I did not get the job.

I continued to look through the column of job openings daily. There were several out of town, but my heart was still leaning toward working at the local YMCA. That job would have been perfect for me.

Soon I went back to the YMCA for my regular swim and while on my way out the door, the manager from the interview was standing nearby. I approached her with a question that would be very important to my future interviews. I asked, "I haven't been to a job interview in ages and yours was my first. Do you have any suggestions for my next interview?"

She said, "Just be yourself." And there it was again, that plain and simple advice.

Slightly puzzled, I said, "I was *myself* and I did not get the job."

She was such a kind, and caring person. She responded, "I still have the notes from that meeting, and I want to take your question very seriously. Let me take a moment and get back to you."

I went home and a few hours later the phone rang. The lady identified herself as the director of membership. "You got the job!" Later it was mentioned they couldn't hire me for the first job because they needed someone right away for long hours and I was still currently working. In the meantime, a part-time position became available due to an employee soon to retire, and they were hoping I would still be available.

I couldn't wait to tell Tony, *everything is going to be alright.*

That evening I thanked God for my new job and one less worry. Then I asked Him for extra strength and energy to work both jobs during the transition. I paused for a moment, took a replenishing breath, and thought that once again another dream had come true with a sprinkle of God's love and His courage. I looked up, my heart full of praise; *I could not have done this without You!*

7

HOPE IS BIGGER THAN FEAR

Every patient who will eventually need an organ transplant is required to have preliminary testing done to prove the individual is strong and healthy enough to withstand the major surgery. Recently, Tony completed all of his tests to confirm whether or not he was a candidate to go on that very extraordinary list. Once again, he waited in the specialist's office for his results, with me by his side. Sometimes the waiting became so intense it took my breath away. I could only imagine how he must have felt.

To break the monotony, I attempted to make a joke, and miserably; it was a dud. He didn't budge, not a laugh, not even a smile, and he appeared a little disturbed by my attempt. Nervously I began to squirm in my chair, wondering what he must be thinking, and the fear he must be experiencing as he sat there, solemnly. We sat in awkward silence; the more time went by, the more the stress became unbearable for both of us.

We sat in the same chairs for many years. Each time we waited for any medical news, we always heard, *'Your test results are the same as the last time. You are still a healthy man. Go home and celebrate,'* with the reminder to stay on the proper diet. Only today was different. I could see his demeanor had changed. He had lost a certain amount of weight and his abdomen protruded from a secondary condition called *'ascites.'*

Sadly, this a condition that usually occurs as the patient's condition worsens toward the last stages.

Waiting for the test results was so grueling this time for both of us, that I knew I had better pull back before I fell into the deep pit of despair; he needed my support. My dear friend, Irene, once reminded me that when in an uncomfortable place, you don't have to *'pitch your tent and camp there forever,'* remember to pray. *"Dear Lord, please guide us with courage while we face many of life's challenges. I understand that courage does not mean the absence of fear, but the strength to continue. We need peace and tranquility in our struggle."*

A few minutes later, I felt peace course through my entire body, the special kind that only God could provide. A welcoming bubble of peace surrounded us. Tony looked in my direction and smiled, as if he felt the serenity, too. Surprisingly, he took his turn at a joke, and he hit a 'homerun' as he often did, and we both laughed. The expression on his face also softened after a good laugh, and almost instantly, he appeared in better spirits. A quiet thought came to mind. It was his delightful sense of humor that caught my heart thirty years ago, and prompted me to say, *'I do.'*

I always appreciated his hilarious sense of humor, and I was often 'all ears' for more of his funny side, starving for something lighter to think about other than medical news. The silliness continued to overcome both of us, a familiar emotional reprieve. I don't know why I was astounded when he said, "Go lock the door. I think we still have enough time for a quickie."

I repeated, "A quickie, Mr. One-Tract-Mind?" We began to banter back and forth, and the rest of our conversation should be left between husband and wife. As we continued to feed each other humorous lines, we both fell into a necessary sea of hilarity.

Abruptly, the doctor walked through the door, and we both sat up straight and cleared our throats. Tony looked very grave, and I'm sure my expression was a mirror image of his. The doctor smiled when he said, "Don't stop laughing on my account; laughter is music to my ears." Although we had permission to continue acting like two goons, we both sat somberly, trying to regain courage, but the fear was overwhelming.

I thought for a second *this poor soul's job is not easy. While he held the answers to the medical reports in his hands, he had to relay the test results to the patients.* The pleasantries and small talk soon ended, and we were down to business.

Yes, the verdict was in; at that moment nothing else mattered, just the results. Our two hearts were pounding anxiously in unison. Suddenly we heard his voice, "While checking over your chart, I noticed it is your birthday today, Tony. Your test results are in, and since I never gave you a gift before, I will give you one today. It's time to add your name to the transplant list."

A moment of silence, and then, seconds later, cold reality set in. What just happened, and did he call this a gift? Although this was what we waited for, the gift of making the list, we understood all too well, there would be a *much worse* stage before the hope of his getting well again.

My dear husband sat very quietly as this news was presented to him. In fact, it took a long time for him to say anything. He looked very brave, almost as if he already knew. Although this was what we were anticipating, there were mixed feelings. A stream of tears started to flow down my cheeks with an unstoppable force. The doctor handed me a box of tissues. "I always keep this handy for the spouse; the patient doesn't need it because they generally already seem to know." He confirmed what I was thinking, and then he asked Tony, "Did you already know?"

He replied, and just simply said, "Yes."

As the doctor went on to explain the particulars, my heart sank, and the room began to spin. I felt dizzy and I looked at Tony with blurred vision from tears. I could see he still looked very strong. Soon the visit ended with the doctor shaking our hands, and reminding us of many follow-up visits. Most important was the reminder to continue diligently, and to always prepare his meals according to his special diet plan. With a shaky voice, "Yes," I agreed. "I understand the importance and I will make sure he does."

While we were making the follow-up appointment for further tests, the specialist and his assistant noticed our serious expressions. The doctor said to his assistant, "Tell them both what you just said to me."

"I thought that you folks have been coming here for many years, and it is about time he went on the list. This is good news; he could get better."

The good doctor nodded in agreement.

Tony was still very quiet, so I spoke as I dried my tears, "Yes, there it is: hope."

We thanked them for the very important reminder that *he will be able to get better*. Those words rekindled the warmth of peace, and we were thankful he was healthy enough for the privilege to be placed on that extraordinary list today.

After we left the office, we walked down, what seemed to be, a very long hallway. The silence was broken when fear set in, and Tony proclaimed, "I could die."

Feeling as if I was just kicked in the stomach for the second time that day, I responded to his announcement with a hug and a reminder, "We didn't come this far for nothing. I believe from this point on, there will be a victory dance. Let's always remember that you may get well again." We clung to each other for support, and then he bravely moved forward to his future.

My mother was with us that day, as she often came for support. As we walked back through the waiting room, sadly, when we came into view, she read our expressions. No words were spoken; we just gave her the literature the doctor gave us to read, and it was titled *Transplant*. She, too, began to cry, and silently hugged us both. Again, no words were spoken, just a quiet understanding as we continued to the next area of the hospital for further testing towards his hope of good health.

As we were leaving the area, to go to the medical imaging department, we were grateful for modern technology and that a transplant meant there was hope. The gloomy moment was broken with a ray of optimism. "Today is your birthday and didn't the doctor say he gave you a gift today?" We all smiled and continued to move forward with a better outlook and hearts full of gratitude for the gift of hope on this very special day, Tony's birthday, and with the reminder that hope is much bigger than fear.

Encouraging Encounters

As we left the clinic, I took a brief moment to look back and recall the many years we had spent waiting in this area, and the concerns, fears, and fond memories of the many people we had the privilege of meeting. They were all at different stages of their illnesses. There were memories of the countless heartfelt stories we had listened to and had shared some of our own. I would cherish those memories of courage as Tony now moved forward to the next level. Sadly, I couldn't seem to pull my eyes away as I continued to gaze, because so many people were critical and in need, waiting for a miracle.

There were people waiting for kidneys, livers, and hearts, and patients with their oxygen tanks by their side while waiting for the gift of lungs. I recall one lady mentioning that she was going on vacation and when I glanced at the oxygen tank at her side, she saw me and said, "Oh, that thing. Nothing stops me from enjoying life." She said she was recently placed on the list, but she doubted they would call her soon. As a matter of fact, she was going to discuss her trip with the specialist. I never saw her again to find out if she was given the go-ahead for her adventure.

One thing I took from her optimism was to make sure Tony and I continued to have special dates on his good days, simple and meaningful day trips to explore what our surrounding area had to offer. I remembered the many encouraging, kind words, just in the nick of time, when we were all dealing with discouragement. There was an illumination of empathy that added great worth to the heart and soul of all who shared these comforting moments. The pick-me-up of meeting these extraordinary people and their families was much more than just conversation to pass the time; these moments were encouraging encounters.

The love and support we received from others back home were appreciated, and here at this clinic, we were with people who shared the truth of this horrendous situation.

I forced myself to think about Tony's next step as we continued toward the unknown future, so grateful there was hope. I turned too quickly and, accidentally smashed my face into the back of his hard head and hurt my nose. That's just what we needed, a 'stooge moment!' I wanted to shout in pain, but I was able to control myself. I wiped my nose and was glad there was no blood, just felt a little foolish. He turned with a disgusted look and, surprisingly, didn't say anything. Instead, he showed mercy by not reprimanding me, because he understood that I was still processing the good news that he would be placed on the Gift of life List.

As I looked around, my mother was peering out the window, looking down at all the hustle and bustle of the city of Toronto. It was nice to have a reprieve, but it was time to get my head on straight and locate the next area. This was going to be an even longer day than we had anticipated. Often, we had to be prepared for unscheduled appointments that may occur on each visit.

We found the medical imaging area. Tony gave them all his information, and we took a seat in the very crowded waiting room on the second floor overlooking the first floor that faced the busy city at street level. I noticed there were tables and a nice refreshment area. We did not have to wait long because they were expecting him. He was moved to yet another area, with another waiting room. I motioned for mom to join us, but she opted to stay where she was and enjoy the view. As we left, I could see she was weary and in need of a moment alone to digest the change of events.

I told her when Tony finished his tests, we would go downstairs, pointing to the coffee shop, for refreshments. She smiled and agreed. As much as we appreciated her support, it was time to encourage her to stay at our house the next time, and watch our dog, Gideon. She could also go for a leisurely swim at our local YMCA close to where we lived. She had already gone through a long journey with my dad's illness and the struggles of becoming a widow. I wanted to spare her as much grief as possible.

Since I am the younger sibling, my mom and sister genuinely want to help when I appear in need. Sometimes, if I protested, my sister would remind me of the 'chain of command' and then we would have a giggle. As long as I could remember, I would say to them, with attitude, *"I've got this. I can do it myself."* Often, I did need their help, but I was just too proud to admit it. When I was in any emotional pain, I could easily go into isolation, and although they could feel me pushing them away, they never left me. They would push back into my life, and without words, instinctively know what was good for me. It was then I needed them the most. They mentioned later that when I went into these moments, it was very painful for them too. I thank God for their love and support.

Tony and I continued to walk, side by side, down the corridor when he whispered again, "I could die."

I felt like I had been kicked in the stomach for the third time that day, and realized, no matter how I felt, he felt much worse. I suppressed my deep emotional pain and comforted him the best I could. I would never truly know how he felt, his physical and emotional pain. He would never know the constant ache of what it feels like to witness someone you love suffer. There was no denying it; we both had a fear of the unknown, and yet had the unspeakable courage to continue. At that moment my love for Tony grew even stronger.

As we went through the door of an unfamiliar area, another truth came to me, one we needed to live by, so I said, "You can get better, and this is what we have been waiting for. Let us remember that from this point on. We cannot go back to the place that was comfortable, but we will adjust through each stage together." He squeezed my hand as we entered the next area. With mixed emotions, we were grateful to move on from where we were toward the hope of a brighter future. We sat for just a moment when we heard his name being called. Once again, the funny version of the pronunciation of our last name would create an icebreaker of necessary humor. I thanked God for so many things and waved to him with a smile of encouragement; it melted my heart when he smiled back.

The attendant mentioned it would take a while, so I went in search of my mother, who was still sitting in the very spot where I had left her. After some refreshments, mom appeared in better spirits, and we returned to the waiting room. Along the way, I noticed a husband and wife and the overwhelming vision of what 'worse' looks like. She was pushing him in a wheelchair; there was nothing left of him but what appeared to be the shell of a man. As she pushed him to the next area, I could sense their great sadness. They both felt me staring and looked at me at the same time. I simply said, "Hello". They smiled and I could see their beautiful spirits in spite of their circumstances. They kept going and I noticed they turned into the very waiting room to which we were headed.

Upon arriving, the couple came into view again, their heads downcast once again. They looked up for only a second and we nodded to each other in silence. My mother took her place beside them, and she had a downcast, grave expression as well. Deep in thought, I am sure my expression mirrored the rest. I went into personal isolation again. I did not want to be interrupted; I just wanted to zone out for awhile, but that was not good because my mind wandered to a worrisome place. In this state, I never noticed there were others in the room. As a matter of fact, I had been slowly isolating myself from everything except the other essentials, like work and church.

Abruptly, we were all awakened from our personal thoughts when a very large, tall man stood up and said to all of us, "You don't need to look so sad. Two years ago, we were just like all of you until I got my transplant. Now look at me; I am strong as a bull." His wife sat next to him and nodded in agreement. Everyone lifted their heads to look at the miracle that stood before us, each with questions, yet thankful he shared there was hope for everyone. My isolation was broken at the right time. There it was, an encouraging encounter, a sense of love, and joy in understanding Tony could get better, just like the living proof of this incredible man standing in front us.

While still in the testing area, a young man said to Tony, who was only a curtain away, "My dad is normally a very quiet man, I wonder what is going on out there? I have never heard him be so verbal."

The man actually stepped out of his personal isolation to comfort all of us. Then he mentioned his son had the same disease, and they were there to support him as he waited for his transplant. We all shared heartfelt stories, which seemed to bring some reprieve from our own pain through our instant support of each other, which, I believe, was sent from above.

Soon we were on our way to yet another area of the hospital; it was time for me to meet with the counsellor for caregivers. While waiting for Tony and mom to return from the restrooms, I met a lovely lady who, I thought, *'had the world by its tail.'* We struck up a conversation and she mentioned she had a transplant three years ago. She was so grateful, that she became a volunteer at the transplant center to encourage others who were fearful. I was amazed because she looked so healthy. Who would have known she was on the other side of the mission?

I mentioned our current situation and wanted my husband to meet her so she could tell him the good news personally. She was happy to help. We visited for a few more minutes when Tony came into view. He looked exhausted and anxiety-ridden from the long day. I couldn't wait for him to hear her news to lighten his spirits as it did mine. She shared her extraordinary story, and as we said our goodbyes, she said she would pray for us. I said we would keep her in our prayers, too.

The joy of meeting two people who received their blessing and shared their success stories was good medicine for all of us. As we moved on to the next area of the hospital, we talked about the fact there was much to be grateful for, and especially for the uplifting moments that I considered to be encouraging encounters!

9

COMFORT FOR THE CAREGIVER

I guided mom and Tony to the last area; it was like walking through a village. After mom saw where we were located, she left to have a breather. I had a few minutes to sit with Tony and digest all that was taking place. We both had reading material, but after reading the same sentence over and over, I realized I was actually struggling to keep my concentration. I placed the book back in my purse, always spine down, as my friend Irene would remind me—a delightful little gesture that will last for a lifetime.

I glanced over at Tony; he looked content reading his magazine, not wanting to be disturbed. I squirmed in my chair to get more comfortable, stretched, and yawned. He looked up and frowned. "Why do you yawn so loudly like a roaring lion? You do know there are other people in the waiting area, not just you. You are so embarrassing!"

With a tad bit of drama, I repeated, "Embarrassing? Sorry I didn't know I was that loud." I looked around the waiting room and it was filling up. While I was in my own little world, I didn't seem to notice.

I reminded myself it is not unusual for couples to become a little snippy when under stress and exhausted. Bickering seemed to have some kind of release for Tony, and most of the time I was willing to comply. Blowing off a little steam would calm him for the later events. Still annoyed, Tony said, "While we are on the subject, you sneeze too loud and are not very ladylike."

"Glad you got that off your chest," I huffed. After another quick glance around, it seemed no one noticed my outburst. Since they were all waiting like we were, I was sure there were other things on their minds besides my body noises.

In any event, someone had to put an end to this ridiculous behavior. "Read your magazine," I whispered rather loudly to make my point. He gave me one last eye roll and stuck his nose back in the magazine. I sank into my chair quietly, a little more mindful of my body noises; or rather, not to make any. I have been to the embarrassing *'school of hard knocks,'* and a yawn or a sneeze wasn't one of the lessons. I come from a family that has cornered the market on humility.

I started to reflect on a really funny story, and just in time for a bit of humor. One day my mother was running late to meet friends and family at a buffet restaurant. It was allergy season. She noticed the tissue box was empty, so she grabbed a roll of toilet paper to make do, and stuffed it in her purse. She met her party and sat down, whereupon the roll of toilet paper not only fell out of her purse, but it also rolled down the aisle for everyone to see. The place became quiet while she scooped it up and sloppily rolled it back up. I remembered thinking that was not just embarrassing, it was hilarious! Mom and I have dozens of stories that could top that one. Well, *'Que Sera, Sera'* (Jay Livingston and Ray Evans, 1956), the Doris Day song from long ago, *'Whatever Will Be, Will Be.'*

Finally relaxed, I gave in to my original thoughts that disrupted my reading in the first place. A few days earlier, after the Sunday church service, an elderly woman approached me on our way out. With a tap on my shoulder, she enquired about my husband's health because she hadn't seen him at church for a while. I assured her everything was alright and wanted to move on. However, instead of brushing her off with pleasantries, I realized she was genuinely concerned and gave her an update. "His condition is changing, and he is slightly starting to go downhill. He is at home sleeping as he is requiring more rest."

She said, "Your role as a caregiver will eventually become very uncomfortable, and you will have no choice but to take care of your husband!"

This comment surprised me, but I replied, "I never thought I had a choice because the marriage vows already prepared me for this day, *'through sickness and in health.'"* Those vows were embedded in my heart forever along with *'for better or for worse.'* I could see my answer satisfied her and the fact that I already knew my role because she smiled approvingly. I love the wisdom of the elderly and some in the community call themselves the 'old guard.' They take it upon themselves to keep us in line, and who doesn't need that once in a while?

I did not know her very well, so I dug a little deeper to find out why she had said that. As it turned out, many years ago she was the caregiver for her husband, and after all her great care, he eventually passed away. She had already lived through the mission and was preparing me for the emotional discomfort of witnessing a loved one suffer from a long-term illness. With a comforting hand on my shoulder, she reminded me to ask her for advice. I appreciated the genuine concern of someone who could empathize and had already walked many miles in the dusty, worn shoes of caregiving. She truly understood my present responsibility and the future role of what was to come. However, I had to admit that my new 'caregiving' shoes hurt and were already uncomfortable.

Transforming from my former life to becoming a caregiver, I realized that no matter how challenging our current situation was for me, emotionally and physically, I totally understood that it was much worse for my husband. People often say, *"This is a mission that we did not ask for."* Caring for a loved one is a mission that, in reality, I did not ask for. However, a verse in the Bible reminded us that, *"He comforts us in all our troubles so that we can comfort others. When they are troubled, we will be able to give them the same comfort God has given us"* (2 Corinthians 1:4, NLT).

This scripture verse, *"give them the same comfort God has given us,"* is a refreshing oasis for all caregivers. In receiving the reprieve of spiritual comfort, we also receive a gift to protect us from camping by bitter waters when the whirlpool of doubt and pain begin to pull us under.

Also, when feeling the pressure, do we reach for earthly or spiritual comforts? I dug a little deeper into my soul, only to realize I had a slight 'monkey' starting to grow on my back. So, instead of complicating my thoughts as I did in the past, I automatically knew to ask God to teach me the difference between earthly and spiritual comfort.

Once again, we were both a little startled at the voice of the attendant trying to pronounce our last name correctly. I noticed Tony had put down his magazine and appeared to be deep in thought and maybe a bit worried. He looked exhausted and I was, too. As I clumsily gathered our belongings, knocking a few things over, he frowned at me. I followed along to the examining room. Wearily rubbing my eyes, I felt a yawn coming on, only this time I knew to suppress it.

It was then the specialist mentioned, "On-sight counselling at the hospital is available for caregivers to have an assessment." He continued, "While Tony is having further tests, it might be a good idea for you to have a one-on-one with the counsellor if needed." I thought it was a great idea and agreed to go. With the nature of his illness, I appreciated any further information that could help. He kindly gave me directions for that meeting. After seeing Tony off, I was on my way to see the counsellor, reminding myself he would be placed on *'the list.'*

En route, I anticipated the conversation would solely be more details about providing for Tony. However, on arrival, I learned it was regarding my own mental and physical health. Apparently, it is common for caregivers to forget about balancing comfort and care for themselves. "Some caregivers end up in worse shape than their loved one if they do not follow this suggestion—don't forget to take care of yourself," the counsellor warned, kindly.

She continued, "People who take on the medical responsibility of their spouse may become exhausted, overwhelmed, and could burn out if they don't take the time to take care of their own personal needs." With a serious tone, "Sadly, some caregivers have entered into a state that is much worse than their loved one's condition." Although I had heard that all before, it was brought to reality by a professional. With a more serious expression, "I understand that your husband will be placed on the transplant list and eventually, the welfare of your husband's life will totally depend on you. That is why it is crucial to follow this important advice, and wise to get into practice now." She repeated, "Take good care of yourself." I thanked her for her professional and personal insight. I had to admit, inadvertently, I was just at the beginning of slightly neglecting to take care of myself, even in my appearance.

The counsellor said, with genuine concern, "Do you have any questions or concerns?"

I hesitated to answer right away. In the past sharing personal feelings was often uncomfortable for me, sometimes revealing weaknesses at the wrong time which was even more discouraging. For a brief moment, I reminded myself she was experienced in this field and had helped many others with her knowledge.

Earlier in the conversation, she had taken the time to share her own personal crisis of the past, which gave me the sense of family-like care. That encouraged me to trust her and value her confidentiality, so I silently commanded myself to speak up. "Yes, thank you for asking. I do have a couple of questions and concerns."

I began to share my personal thoughts. "Physicians, often remind us there will be a *'much worse'* before a *'-better.'* I find that particular statement to be incredibly overwhelming because often it appears that we are already at the threshold of *'worse.'* Doctors also mentioned *'the revolving door.'*

"Yes." She knew what I meant, and she continued, "The *'revolving door'* expression is referring to the time when the patient nears the transplant, and they often spend more time in the hospital than not."

"Exactly, and that thought is very unsettling." I continued, "Furthermore, there is the grim realization that a small percentage of patients never receive their transplant, due to timing. Several of us wanted to become live donors, but we were not a match. So, in waiting, it is obvious there will be a time when he will totally lose his independence and, in some ways, I will, too."

Unable to fight the tears any longer, "Frequently, I prayed to stay in the moment and not think too far ahead about *the worse* to come, or *the revolving door*, then cold reality kicked me in my soul." I could no longer fight the sting of holding back my tears, and the flood began.

With shaky hands, I reached for the tissue box she was holding out to me and accidentally dropped the box on the floor. We both reached for it; I pulled back so we wouldn't bang our heads together like a couple of stooges.

She handed the box to me for the second time. I scooped it up quickly and with a slight quiver in my voice, I continued, "I understand the weight of his illness will eventually become much heavier than my own two hands could possibly carry. I may have to rely on help from others."

With an eyebrow slightly raised, she said, "You know it is okay to ask for help."

With uncertainty, "Is it okay?" I questioned.

She looked curious. "Why do you ask?"

I sniffled a little and then, feeling a little more at ease, "Well, lately, I seem to have some sort of block when it comes to asking for help. There has to be some kind of balance when asking, not to overload one person, family, or friend. They all seem to have their own crosses to bear already."

"Do you have children?"

"Yes, we have a daughter and a son that I treasure as two gifts from God. They were very young when their dad began to show signs of his illness."

I continued, "They are grown adults now and are a great support to us as they continue to develop skills to understand our unique family situation. However, they are both planning to be married in the midst of all of this, two months apart. Christina and Steven are very traditional, and we already love their spouses-to-be. They will be moving out soon to have lives of their own, about which I am thrilled. However, it is one more change to adjust to—the empty nest syndrome. Since there has been a 'yo-yo' of ups and downs, I strive for some form of family stability, which is very important to me."

She smiled, "I have children, too, and I totally get it."

"Thank you for understanding."

"There is one more concern. Recently another situation arose. After twenty-eight years of service, I will be losing my job. Our place of business will be closing its doors forever in just one year. I will miss our little store and the employers were very accommodating to our family situation. I was hoping to find work before my job ended in hopes of easing the pain. So I have already been hired and started work at a new job"

"You are experiencing many changes."

"Yes, so many. Do you think that might explain the ache I have, a weight deep in my soul that I cannot identify, similar to being dropped from the giant hill of a roller coaster? Almost a sense of fear. In the Bible, Paul talked about the *'thorn in his side'* and often I refer to this feeling of discomfort as the *'thorn in my stomach'*" (2 Corinthians 12:7, NLT).

She nodded and, with a smile, added, "I, too, am a believer."

"In the past, Tony and I were both ambitious people. We enjoyed various accomplishments and all life had to offer in the eyes of a young couple. Then, with this wake-up call, the years have disappeared before us and we will be adjusting to additional roles not only as husband and wife but patient and caregiver. I hope to eventually gain the strength of two people when it is needed. We have talked about his feelings many times, and again we both understand that his part in this is much worse than mine. Then we remind each other not to dwell on this *'worse'* to come. We have both become very supportive of each other.

"Through the many years, we have shared countless experiences and trials. It is comforting to know any cracks that were in our foundation have been sealed for life. *For better or worse* we are in this for the long haul, together. Our pastor said, 'There are three important words that start with the letter *'P'*: *Pray, Prepare and have a Plan.'* I attend an old-fashioned church that has become a second home to me. It sports a giant cross that lights up in the evening and is a delight in our small town. The lights in the cross went out once and several of the townsfolk let the pastor know; even though they weren't members, they appreciated the light, too."

As she wrote something on her chart, I took a moment to glance out the window. While looking down at the busy streets of Toronto, I observed the busyness of the city like a hamster on the wheel of life. I started to daydream and remembered the caption of the old commercial from more than forty years ago. The catchphrase was *'Calgon take me away.'* Although the manufacturers were merely selling bubble baths, they were also selling a form of comfort, a sense of getting away from it all. I thought *if only that was all it took to wash away our troubles; life would be so much simpler as it had been many years ago. In all our busyness of life, did we even notice and appreciate the simpler life?*

She stopped writing and spoke, "We covered several matters and during most of the conversation, I noticed a strength you already have that will continue to help you tremendously on your mission and will become a great comfort to you." She paused for a second, "That is your noticeably strong faith." She added, "I rely on that strength, too."

I thought for a moment of the volume of caregivers she must have helped along the way and the blessing that she had a strong faith, too. She continued, "Spending time in prayer will be your guide and a great comfort to you." She handed me her card, "As new issues arise, call for support anytime."

"Thank you very much for your kindness and care, it really meant a lot."

"One last reminder, *'ask and you shall receive,'* and not just when the load becomes too heavy."

She hugged me goodbye and as grateful as I was for her support and wisdom, I knew I would probably never see her again because Toronto was just too far away. This meeting was very important because I realized that advice from a professional was essential. I didn't want to rely too heavily on any one person and bog them down with my troubles. I realized asking for professional help was not a weakness but a source of strength, especially when there are so many educated counsellors to help with proper advice.

Feeling emotionally renewed, I wandered back to the original area where we were to reunite. Looking around I could see they had not yet returned. I was only away for forty-five minutes, but his tests often took a bit longer. The hospital chapel was nearby, so a visit there for a few minutes would be refreshing. On entering I could feel peace as I sat down. I began to pray for Tony and his test. I gave thanks for the insight of the counsellor. Her words suddenly came to mind that God would be my comfort.

I began to think, *when treading in troubled waters, do we reach for spiritual comfort or earthly comfort?* I had to admit to myself, disappointingly, my earthly comfort was clear and that was white wine. I asked God to show me the way to spiritual comfort so as not to rely on temporary earthly comforts for support. I prayed, *"Please help me, when searching for comfort, to rely on You."*

After thanking God for help and for listening, I left the chapel feeling slightly worn out, and wandered back to meet Tony and my mother. While deep in thought, I banged my shoulder into the partition that separated the coffee shop from the hospital. When I came back to reality, I rubbed my shoulder and thought that I need to be more alert as there is no comfort in getting hurt from exhaustion. I purchased three coffees and a light snack and carried them back to where I was to meet my family, but they still had not arrived.

I sat in a comfy chair with the book I brought; only once again my mind started to wander, and I gave in to my thoughts. I was thinking about the first time I heard the *'comfort prayer,'* about receiving God's comfort in order to give to others the same measure of comfort He gives us. It was when my mom, my sister, Cheryl, and I were standing at dad's bedside, trying to comprehend this would be the last time we would see him on earth. The chaplain prayed with our family and quoted the comfort prayer. After he finished, I looked up and noticed how weary my mother and sister looked because they had just 'camped out' at the hospital for the last ten days of dad's life to make sure he was comfortable.

I was born and raised in the United States but now live in Canada. So, to support my family I would cross the Peace Bridge to be by their side every day, allowing myself to indulge in crocodile tears all the way over the bridge. Once in the US, there was always the reminder to be strong for my mom and sister, and the flood would stop automatically. I would return home the same way and the bridge was my alone time to release stress. I would come and go every day, and return home to tend to the comforts of my young family. It was no surprise, after my dad's passing, that just the sight of the bridge caused me panic attacks.

Eventually, I was able to overcome them and able to drive over the bridge again, but it took a long time.

Minutes after the chaplain left the room, my mom announced, "I have to go to the cafeteria and have a cheeseburger." I understood immediately; every family has its own version of comfort, so off to the snug warmth of cafeteria food we went. Although my mom found comfort in the cheeseburger, it was only temporary relief, and she went back into a state of shock. Pain and grief overwhelmed me at the thought that my parents were high school sweethearts. My heart was grieving for both of us. The empty space left without him was unbearable.

Suddenly, a nice person appeared and introduced herself. She spoke with such empathy, "I was in the next room when your dad passed away and I couldn't help but overhear your agonizing grief when you cried out, 'I don't have a dad anymore!'"

Puzzled, I remembered saying that, but I would not have thought anyone else was listening. She continued, "When I heard you sob, it broke my heart and all I wanted to do was to find you and give you a hug." Her sincerity overwhelmed me, so I reached out, and we embraced. I thanked her for her thoughtfulness and told her she must have been heaven-sent. I received great comfort from a complete stranger, an earthly angel.

We spent many moments in the hospital chapel because my family knew the importance of letting go and letting God comfort us. Although my mother's earthly comfort was a cheeseburger, she would also find comfort in topping off the meal with a hot fudge sundae. My sister's comfort would be scouting out the nearest pizzeria. However, my comfort food has always been chips and dip. My sister mentioned French fries are also high on her list of 'go to' comfort foods. She wanted to get a little black book and journal all the great pizzas or French fries places she found while looking for comfort in the middle of a crisis. As amusing as it sounds, it sure seemed to do the trick, if only for the moment.

The *'monkey on my back'* was trying to mature, beginning with a simple glass of wine which sounds innocent enough. However, it started to stretch and extend its limits. *Isn't it better to nip a growing concern in the bud?* I knew I had to find another comfort that was not habit-forming, and healthier. Tony arrived and we sat quietly for a moment. He appeared tired, and I noticed his skin tone looked a little greyer and his eyes a bit sunken. I said, "I missed you while you were gone."

He said, "Me too."

Mom arrived and we all enjoyed a break with our lovely raisin tea biscuits and coffee. We continued to eat in silence, as we were all a little weary. Our day had started at 3:30 am!

On our bus ride home, I mentioned my encounters and I admitted the changes I needed to make. He said, "From what I have witnessed, I think you drink very moderately."

"Well, yes, I am in that range, but I only do it in the evening when I am in pain, and I do not think it is right. I don't want to develop a dependency. My goal is to form a new support system to take care of myself, including an awareness of earthly comforts. As our situation becomes more challenging, I will have already developed a strong foundation so it does not crack under the weight of what we will endure."

"I know you best, and I believe you already have that strong foundation; you will be fine"

I smiled and kissed him. "Thanks for your support." We settled into our comfortable chairs for the long ride ahead of us and cuddled closely. We both gazed out the bus window knowing there was much more to come. The most important key for the caregiver is relying on God's comfort and when we receive it, we are not meant to keep it to ourselves; it is a gift we are given to share.

10

Always Ask

"*Grateful*" would be the perfect word to describe the welcoming comfort of coming home after a long day of travel and appointments. With a mighty yawn and an extensive stretch, Tony opted to watch television upstairs in our bedroom and relax. Before he left the room I asked if he would like a snack. He said, "No. No thank you."

I noticed lately; his appetite was declining which concerned me. "I will be up shortly after I finish a few chores, Love."

Quickly I glided through all that was necessary to get ready for the next workday and then I crawled, wearily, into bed next to him. He rolled in my direction and smiled, "I am so glad I have you by my side through all of this."

I smiled back, "I am glad to be by your side." He reached for my hands, kissed them both, and then squeezed them tight.

As we cuddled, I said, "It really is a blessing that you were placed on the list today.

He agreed.

Optimistically I said, "After all, this is what we were waiting for, right?" hiding my emotional pain as I thought of the unknown of what comes next. I continued, "What was also significant to me was when you mentioned to the doctor you were not in any pain, just very fatigued most of the time."

Sleepily, he added, "Yes that is true."

I was concerned about his level of comfort, so it was a relief to have that assurance. "It hurts me deeply to think you may be in any pain."

"No worries, just tired."

"When the doctor mentioned you were no longer able to work a long time ago, he was surprised you were still working." This had been an ongoing occasional subject; because, as we both continued to work, we felt a sense of normalcy. A few weeks ago, he took me by surprise when he admitted the workday was becoming more of a challenge. We both knew eventually he would have to stop working completely, but he had not yet set a date. Delicately, I said, "I understand you will know when it is time to make that decision." I barely finished the sentence as I watched him fall into a deep sleep. I continued to gaze at him as I pondered the fact he could still muster up enough energy to get him through the work day.

I rolled over and shut off the television and the light. In the darkness my mind wandered to the grim image of the lady pushing her husband down the corridor in a wheelchair; the dismal expressions on their sweet faces haunted me. It was a reminder of the harsh and accurate comment that my husband's condition would only worsen, too. The vision of them and what our future would become stung my heart. Lately, as his condition was already in the process of worsening, his physical appearance was changing at a more drastic rate. His belly was retaining water and looked very uncomfortable; his arms and legs looked thin which was disturbing to me. There was a procedure that could remove the fluid, but it was only temporary, and the water retention would eventually come back.

Since the days were so full of many things to do, it took my mind off our troubles. However, it was at night that sadness and worry would weigh heavily on my heart and could sometimes make sleeping difficult. Although the Bible reminds us to cast our cares and worries on the Lord, often I found that verse to be easier said than done. I began to pray. I asked, *"As he loses his strength, is it possible for me to gain the strength of two people with Your help to carry us? I can only imagine things getting worse; we need a stronger foundation to truly stay in each moment of the day."*

I prayed, also, for the couple that had been ahead of us at the hospital with all their issues. I prayed for comfort for the husband, and compassion and strength for his lovely wife. Suddenly, the direction of my thinking changed, and I began to recall all the encouraging encounters we were blessed with that day. What stood out the most was the hopeful reminder that he could get better. *"Thank you, Lord, for so many things, and I can feel Your warmth and peace."* I mentioned how important rest was for both of us to be refreshed and renewed; a good night's sleep would take some of the edge off our daily mission. My heart was comforted and that was the last thing I remembered because I, too, fell into a very deep sleep.

Upon waking, even though I had proper rest, I was still a little fatigued from the previous day. I glanced over at Tony continuing to enjoy a well-deserved rest, so I didn't disturb him. At the bottom of our bed, warming our feet, lay faithful old Gideon as always, sprawled out and taking more than his share of the bed. I love him dearly and am grateful for his friendship. Today he is scheduled to work at one of our local retirement homes before I go to work. Although he continued to be a volunteer in our community as a therapy dog, he, too, would have to stop working as life continued to unfold. But for now, I had the privilege of holding his leash as he worked his personal magic. He brought joy to the community with his adorable ways.

I am a bit clamorous when I wake up, so I tried to be considerate as I padded down the hallway to let Gideon outside. While on the way, I banged my toe into the floorboards and screamed inside myself so as not to wake up Tony. As usual, Gideon just watched me with his sweet face. Just the sight of him let me know everything was going to be alright. After letting him out, I prepared his breakfast, made coffee, and gathered my devotional books. When I opened the door again, Gideon came in wagging his tail. He took his usual spot by my feet and ate his kibbles while I sat, cozy in a wingback chair.

The scripture verse attached to my devotional reading was Matthew 7:7 (NIV), *"Ask and it will be given to you; seek and you will find; knock and it will be opened to you."* I wasn't planning on a confession this morning, but it was time to 'fess up' and step up. I mentioned in prayer about earthly comforts and that my vacation from pain was the occasional white wine. Admitting our weaknesses isn't always easy, but God is great with the big stuff and the little. I finished my prayer time and got ready for the day, with a plan to have a stronger foundation for all future endeavors. That included clearing out the clutter of life and anything that saps the necessary strength required to be the best caregiver possible.

While driving to work, I remembered again our pastor saying that when you pray, prepare and have a plan. I parked my car. As I was entering the building, an elderly couple looked like they were waiting for me. As I came closer, I realized I had never seen them before. The wife declared, "You drove into the parking lot too quick and scared us!" I looked over at her quiet husband as he nodded his head in agreement.

I really did not feel like a confrontation at that moment. However, I guessed it was my turn to speak as they both seemed to be studying my reaction. "I am very sorry I scared you, and thank you for taking the time to tell me. I will be more mindful from now on." I smiled in a friendly manner to keep the peace.

They didn't smile back and looked shocked at my answer. Their mouths, oddly, hung frozen in an open position. I questioned, "Now what's wrong?" They both spoke at the same time. I didn't know which one to pay attention to, so I kept spinning my head back and forth. What I gathered from the commotion was they had to correct others in the past about their driving skills or lack of it, as well. Upon mentioning this, the accused would get annoyed at them and conclude with a *mind your own business*. I said, "I hope I didn't disappoint either of you." I found them both to be very amusing. At this point I couldn't help but giggle, and so did they. The situation became light and friendly, and I wished them a better day as we waved in passing.

I ran through the door, up the stairs, clocked in on the dot, and then wandered by the Human Resources office. Suddenly I got a notion that I should muster up the courage, and share my concerns with Silvana, our HR person, thinking how much I would miss her when our store closes. We were blessed the day she came to work with us. As time moved on, I considered her a friend and valued her opinion. Mindlessly, I found myself knocking on the door that was already open. She looked up from her paperwork and I could see she looked very busy. "Would it be possible some time and, hopefully, today, to have a chat? Lately, I feel like my ship keeps trying to sink and I can barely keep it afloat much longer." I was very serious at this point.

With sisterly concern, she replied, "How about right now?"

I was relieved to get this off my chest, so I sat down immediately, and took my place across from her.

I shared all about our current situation at home: the pending transplant, the changes with grown kids soon getting married, the empty nest, and the sudden change in occupation while working two jobs. Skipping to the chase, "Most of the time I struggle with intense emotional pain that is so grueling." While feeling a bit ashamed and casting my eyes downward at the thought, I confessed, "In the evening only, I have been drinking white wine to take a break from my pain. I have a strong sense this is not a good idea, and the pain only seems to intensify the next day anyway." Continuing with a feeling of heat on my face, "It is my personal *get away* like a mini vacation from my troubles; if only for that moment, it relieves my severe emotional pain. When I have mentioned this to others, apparently there is some thought that I am in a normal range of moderate alcohol consumption. However, that enabling gesture doesn't help matters. I know it is not a good idea and I want to stop this before it becomes a bigger problem."

In a caring, nonjudgmental way she asked, "How much are you drinking?"

Feeling at ease and that God had sent me to the right person, I continued, "Well, at first it was all quite innocent, but soon after, I went from one night a week, to two nights, and then to five nights. On the nights that I wasn't drinking, I was thinking about it. Do you think I should go to an AA (Alcoholics Anonymous) meeting before this becomes a much bigger problem?"

Her opinion was very important to me, and I trusted her answer to help guide me through. She replied, "It wouldn't hurt?" Although I already knew the answer to my question, I appreciated her suggestion, casual and to the point, "it wouldn't hurt."

I thanked her and stood up to get to work. As I was leaving, I said, "Then it is settled. I will call tonight after work and thank you again for your support."

She said, "It is part of my job."

"I always forget that, because you are so naturally helpful."

As I moved a little quicker to get to work, she said, "Please let me know the outcome."

As I ran down the hallway, I replied with a fading voice, "You know it," and hurried down the stairs to the fashion area where I loved to work, hoping no one noticed my slight delay.

From time to time, customers would ask, "What are you going to do now that your store is closing?"

I thought, *what I need to do is stop cringing every time someone asks the same question. I feel bad enough without everyone reminding me, although I knew they were asking because they genuinely cared and were concerned.*

Everyone in management already knew I had found a new job; they thought it would be best if people found out, naturally, which did not take very long in a small community. Although I was so grateful to find a new job, I still cared about the other employees who would soon, if not already, start making plans for new employment. Often, during lunch break, I shared with the others about a place in town that could help in the search for work with such things as resumes, courses, and preparing for an interview. The day went by fast as we were very busy. There were the questions of the lovable townsfolk, and our wondering where each of us was going to go next. Sometimes it seemed there was just too much going on all at once.

After dinner, I mustered up some courage and called a chapter of AA. To my surprise, the pleasant lady who answered the phone said there was a meeting scheduled for the very next evening and I was welcome to join them. I was elated. The chapter I chose was in a town nearby. I decided to go to an AA chapter out of town for privacy. I just wasn't ready to be found out and was concerning myself with being judged at this point. I committed myself, said I would be there for sure, and thanked her for her kindness. I sat back in my chair and, oddly, stared at the receiver for a moment, trying to comprehend the next step. I thanked God for the courage that I had even done it. As I hung up the phone, it rang and startled me. It was my mom and when I explained everything, she was very supportive.

That next evening came all too quickly. I hesitated slightly before entering the church where the meeting was being held, and questioned again, *Am I doing the right thing?* I pushed myself forward. As I entered, everyone was so hospitable and welcoming. One by one, they introduced themselves. They understood and genuinely wanted to help. As the evening progressed, they all shared their personal stories of why they were there, and in listening to their testimonies, I gained confidence. I felt comforted, hopeful, and, especially, not alone. I was comfortable enough to take my turn at confessing and stood up to share my personal story, too. They all listened to my moment of truth. When the meeting was over, they gave me a very helpful book which I eventually read from cover to cover.

The next day I knocked on Silvana's door and, with a smile, she immediately invited me in. I sat down, enthusiastic to share the whole story as briefly as possible because I didn't want to take up too much of her time. After sharing my experience, I told her about one thing that stood out the most, the thing that I will always remember about that meeting. When I was ready to leave, with my hand on the doorknob, a very humble lady approached me, removed a pin from her lapel, and placed it in my hand. She said she was 12 years sober, and the pin she placed in my hand was given to her the first time she came to a meeting, and she wore it for 12 years until that very day. The pin was an angel, and my hand trembled with the love and care that I felt at that moment. Tears rolled down my cheeks. I thanked her for such a special gift and she hugged me.

As I continued to share the story with my friend, I said that without her answer *'it wouldn't hurt,'* I would have never gone for outside help, and she was right, *it didn't hurt.* To show my gratitude, I placed the angel pin in the palm of her hand. "It would mean a lot to me if you kept this angel pin. I will never forget your kindness, and for listening to me during a time when I was feeling very small and unheard." We both had a sparkle in our eyes trying to hold back the tears. I took a new step forward and thanked God for pointing me in the right direction of people and places to ask for help. Although asking for help was not one of my strong points, I was grateful I did, and when I went back to work, I had a sense of liberty in the verse, *"Ask, and it will be given to you; seek, and you will find; knock, and the door will be opened to you"* (Matthew 7:7, NIV).

The test of time proved that the results were mighty. I cut way back on my alcohol consumption and disciplined myself, too. Recently, a good friend asked me if some of the problem might be guilt because Tony can never drink alcohol for the rest of his life. My answer was brief and simple, "Yes," also with the understanding that he needed me to be there for him, completely. Although I never went back for a second AA meeting at the little church, I would always have a fond affection for the kind people I met there. Eventually, I gave the helpful book they gave to me to another who was in need.

I did have a second meeting, only this time it was with God, and we met several times a day. 1 John 4:14 (NLT) reminds us that we are confident that He hears us whenever we ask for anything that pleases Him. I began to develop an ever stronger level of trust in God and our relationship seemed to soar from that point on. Whenever I faced any dilemma, I would pray first and ask for His opinion, and He would lead me in the right direction to be the best I could be for Tony. I worshiped and thanked Him often while appreciating how gracious He had been in our crisis. Then I looked up to Him and winked because I realized that to me the acronym for AA is to *always ask*.

11

A Gentle Nudge

A series of warm and fuzzy moments flooded my thoughts continuously for about three days. It was like when someone says their whole life flashes before their eyes. This was the same, yet different. The pleasant memories gave my mind a break from dwelling on medical issues, like emotional protection, for what was to come.

Many happy moments had occurred in the past year, joyful memories to cherish: simple day trips, sitting by the lake and enjoying a date square at Niagara-on-the-Lake, visiting Olcott Beach and dining at Gordy Harper's Bazaar, enjoying an ice cream cone on a giant swing while appreciating a beautiful view at Lewiston, a ride on a train at an amusement park, reading a good book while relaxing, and many picnics along the Niagara River. What they all had in common was a body of water, great food, and a sense of peace that felt like we were on vacation, only we hadn't gone very far from home.

As time moved on, I wished the great memories would not fade, but continue to be an important part of our emotional health and well-being. After basking in those thoughts, I felt a longing for more good memories, so I began to talk to God as my Friend. *"Is it possible to actually go back to a familiar safer place in time? It is getting closer to the closing of our store and the anticipation of the mission. I trust You will carry us both through, and please teach me to truly give my worries to You. I need help with that area. Also, I am looking for another temporary reprieve from my thoughts and hope to have a few more good memories to hold on to."*

While I was praying, I felt an undeniable sense of peace and warmth coursing through my veins. I must have prayed in the express lane because the answer came so quickly. An uncanny thought overwhelmed me to go back and visit the old house where I had grown up. Years ago when driving through the small village of Kenmore, I never missed an opportunity to park in front of that house and savor all of its memories.

The last time I parked in front of it, I imagined our Christmas tree in the front window, the real pine tree my family and I carefully chose for our holiday. Artificial trees were just starting to be the new hit of the season, and as I recall they were either white or silver. Eventually, we opted for the silver one which sat in the centre of our family room.

I could still picture our dog, Sparky, in that window, and it brought to mind the Christmas my mom and I will never forget. It all began when she finished wrapping the presents by one in the morning on December 25th and went to bed. She was so tired she didn't hear the culprit. Our Sparky, a gentle German Shepherd, was sneaky. He quietly went into the living room and proceeded to unwrap all the presents. The grand finale was when he lifted his leg up against the tree. It was a cold winter night. In his doggy mind, he must have thought we were being considerate and had brought the tree inside just for him. He was dearly loved by our whole family, so it was no surprise mom didn't stay angry with him for too long.

While still thinking about those fond memories, I called my friend, Irene, and mentioned this notion of mine, about visiting the old house, thinking it to be rhetorical. However, she enhanced the situation with an award-winning question. "On the next visit, why don't you knock on the door and ask if you can go inside?" Pausing, while trying to digest what she had just said, I passed it off as kidding.

I started to chuckle. "No, you can't do that, can you?"

She laughed. "Why not? I did it not too long ago. "Surprisingly, she wasn't kidding.

I was amused by her slightly intimidating question, plus the fact she had already been inside her old house. After enjoying a lovely conversation, we said our goodbyes, and the conversation finished with, "Maybe I will give some thought to that unusual request."

My friend is a little older than I am and she is often equipped with a fresh idea or two to motivate us. She ended the conversation with, "Talk to you tomorrow. Bye, bye." She has a pleasant way of saying *bye, bye*, almost like spiritual music.

After hanging up the phone, I shook my head, laughing at how outlandish she can be sometimes. She is a very proper English woman with impeccable manners. When we go out for lunch together, I watch her carefully so I can follow her lead, because she is very ladylike. She doesn't even crinkle her napkin, and I admire that about her. Personally, for me, you can just *fill the trough* and I will eat anything and everything if it is cooked properly. I have to remember to blot my mouth because I generally end up wearing my food, as the old expression goes, *'to save a snack for later'*. My friend doesn't seem to mind that I often appear as though I have never eaten before, and the more I enjoy the food the more noise I make as well.

When enjoying a night out at the movies, I am often glad when the lights go out because I can't cram the popcorn in my mouth fast enough. By the time I get home to put on my PJs, I have to admit, there's popcorn still falling off me and sometimes even in my bra. No problem, my sheltie, Gideon, is more than happy to clean up the morsels that have fallen to the floor. It is interesting that my dear friend never has a hair out of place and is always properly groomed; while in the rush, my hair often looks like an unmade bed. The one thing that stands out most is her uncanny way of offering a gentle nudge when needed.

While caught up in the reverie, the phone rang, startling me. "Would you like to go to our favorite spaghetti house for their Monday special?"

It was my mother and I replied enthusiastically, "All you-can-eat spaghetti. Twist my arm. I will invite Christina & Jay and we will meet you at five-ish tomorrow." Christina is my daughter and my oldest. She has always been the calm in my storm, but of course, she is a firstborn and often they are already born with mature qualities. She is very petite, has a sweet disposition, and a winning smile. I always loved to bake Christmas cookies with my little girl, now a grown young lady. Jay is her fiancé, and I couldn't ask for anyone better to become my son-in-law; he is also a firstborn and they make a lovely couple.

Spaghetti night was always a family favorite. The restaurant has changed very little over the years, and the price is still like a step back in time. The sauce is scrumptious and the same for about 50 years. They have a great menu; the pizza and chicken wings are incredible. Christina had been there many times with us in the past so was as thrilled to go as I was. She said her fiancé liked Italian food, too, so they were looking forward to joining our fun family evening.

While dinner with my family was great, one thing was lurking my mind: the answer to my prayer. The restaurant in Buffalo was only two turns away from my old house. The opportunity to follow through with my friend's idea could be as soon as tomorrow. Wow! It flabbergasted me how prayers can be answered so quickly sometimes. The small village I looked forward to seeing again was Kenmore, not far from the restaurant. How uncanny the way this was falling into place when I was only just thinking about it an hour ago.

The conversation about mustering up some courage to boldly knock on a complete stranger's door and invite myself in, sounded a little silly to me, who had already spent a lifetime of inanely embarrassing moments on a regular basis. The suggestion instantly started to discourage me, and the *'what ifs'* swarmed through my head. *Why do I love to exhaust myself by overthinking things that generally turn out to be wonderful? After all, I did ask God, so how could this go wrong?*

During a crisis years ago, my friend and next-door neighbor asked me, "How many times do the unnecessary worries of *'what if'* come true?" As I thought hard about this important question, I responded, "Never." I was concerned about *what if* they closed the door in my face when I asked to come into their home. Hopefully, that *what-if* would be added to the list of previous *what-ifs* that never happened. My dear friend Nancy's wise words from years ago helped me now.

After a good night's sleep and a long day at work, I rounded up my group and we crossed the bridge from Fort Erie to Buffalo to enjoy the dinner I had dreamed about all day. After a lovely meal at the Spaghetti House, we drove to Kenmore to an old ice cream parlor that still exists from my childhood. When I was a newspaper girl, I would save a little extra money from my earnings and ride my 'banana' bike to this same place to purchase a Mexican sundae of vanilla ice cream, chocolate sauce, Spanish peanuts, and, of course, whipped cream and a cherry. Another special memory to cherish.

We entered the old ice cream parlor, and, to my surprise, everything was exactly as I remembered it, including the old-fashioned pictures of celebrities on the wall. The sundae was so large we asked for extra spoons as we were already full from dinner. It was nice just to share. Now it was time to proceed toward the old house. I was so excited. As we drove down Delaware Avenue in historic Buffalo, off to the right was my old grade school, Washington Elementary; the other school I attended was Roosevelt, both named after presidents, one of which is still in operation. Then we passed an old restaurant that used to be called *Watson's*, home of the most amazing chocolate. During holidays they would bring back some of their original treats.

A left turn and there it was—the old house. I started to lose my nerve so I lingered in the car until I could muster up some courage. I tried to be considerate and not to take too long to decide; I had to remember I wasn't alone in the car. My daughter, Christina, and her fiancé, Jason, were with me and kind enough to appease my unusual request. Suddenly, *what if* came back with a vengeance.

The discomfort I felt had the same effect as a memory that occurred almost 50 years ago at our community pool, the kind of childhood memory that is so haunting, you would like to forget it ever happened.

Well, the local pool was just a few blocks from the old house. It was going to be my first attempt to go down the 'big' slide. As I recall, it was a blazing hot day. There was a long lineup for the big slide which extended halfway around the pool. I could still remember my friend and I skipping down the street with our swim gear. It was a delightful, old-fashioned neighborhood with trees that 'umbrella' the whole street, providing shade on a hot summer day.

While waiting our turn, my little friend thought it was important to warn me of any mishap she had ever seen or heard of, including several serious problems on this suddenly treacherous slide. The wait was long, so she had plenty of time to scare me to death. I had anticipated a fun activity, not the nightmare she was describing. I was only six years old at the time, so it was no surprise that looking down the barrel of this slide suddenly took on the appearance of being twice the size. My knees started to buckle. I put on the brakes and opted to back out. The poor lifeguard was sympathetic and had to get that long line to back up. I could hear snickers from the other kids. Of course, my friend reminded me for years of what she thought, was a funny moment. I have to admit, if it had happened to her, I would have reminded her, too.

Finally, I made the decision to accept my friend's challenge, remembering that when I eventually did go down the slide, it was a lot of fun.

With a bit of drama, I said to Christina and Jason, "Keep your cell phones handy in case of an emergency, because they could be weirdoes."

My daughter, slightly amused, said, "Mom, they are not the weirdoes, you are, and what an imagination you have."

Slightly bruised, I said, with attitude, "Me a weirdo?"

She continued, "Yeah, and furthermore, who would attempt to do something like this anyway?"

I quickly reminded her, "Well, Irene did, and so will I!"

I suddenly gained the courage I didn't have moments earlier. I pushed the car door open and marched myself straight up to the front door. After all, I did live here first! I walked up the rickety old steps with shaky knees, where, years ago, I would sit for hours and do my homework. With trembling hands, I reminded myself I was not *Dorothy* going to meet the *Wizard of Oz*. I stood in front of the door straightening my jacket and nervously running my hand through my hair. Finally, I reached up and knocked.

Pause. No answer. I didn't come this far for nothing. I knocked again. To my surprise, an adorable little boy answered the door. I said, "Is your mother home?"

He asked, "Who are you?"

I smiled, and said, "My name is Debbie and I used to live here," and started to explain.

The mother appeared immediately, pushed the door open and said, with a big smile, "I'm sorry I didn't come to the door. I thought you might be a salesman. They often come to my door." Kindly, she said, "Do you want to come in and see *your* house?" *Wow! That was easy, what a waste of time worrying.*

We quickly introduced ourselves and with a nostalgic expression, Janine said, "By the way, I, too, just visited my childhood house last month." I thought *how uncanny, first Irene visits her childhood house, then this lady does, and now me. There must be some sort of epidemic starting.*

Enthusiastically she waved her hand, and said, "Come inside." It was like walking through a dream. I was *actually* standing in *my* living room with all its memories.

I couldn't wait to thank Irene for her gentle nudge and to think I thought it was an unrealistic idea. Pointing to the area in *our* living room and the space by the window, I said, "This is where we displayed our Christmas tree every year."

She smiled and said, "We do, too."

"That is the corner where we kept our old record player. There were no CDs or I-Pods, only small records called '45s' with only one song, or albums that played several songs."

I could still picture the Christmas albums with covers that looked like wrapped Christmas presents. I had looked forward to hearing those old albums for many years. That was also where we left homemade sugar cookies and milk for Santa, and a carrot for Rudolph. I still look forward to the first snowfall and the first sound of Christmas music. I thought of memorable holidays, especially when our grandparents were alive. They made the holidays so special with their old-fashioned recipes, snuggles, and love.

We walked through the kitchen. There was the breakfast nook where my dog, Sparky, would lie on the table and wait for us to come home. My mother never had to shoo him off, because he jumped down before we came in, as if we didn't know. Sparky was able to reach up to the table and, on occasion, steal food. I recalled a time mom called dad to the table for a steak dinner, only for dad to arrive and say, "Where is the steak?"

Suddenly, my eyes started to water at the memory of our family pet, even though we have enjoyed several pets since he passed. Dad loved that dog so much that he called Sparky 'his son', especially since the house was filled with only females: my mom, my sister, Cheryl, and me. When dad realized what had happened to his dinner, he kindly said, "June, do we still have any *Sahlen* hot dogs in the fridge? I will be happy with that." He patted Sparky on the head and said, "Hope you enjoyed that, son." He was more than a pet; he was a family member. Mom still does not think that story is funny.

One last look out the back window and I could envision Sparky playing in the yard. I pictured many birthday parties there, especially the cherry cake with cherry icing. We would clean out the garage, so my sister and our friends could have sleepover parties there in the summer. At the time, our small town was like living in *Mayberry*, the town on the *Andy Griffith* show. When I mentioned this, Janine said things had changed in 50 years, and no one should be out after dark.

Suddenly reality set in. "Oh no. I was having so much fun I forgot my family is in the car. I have taken so long I hope they are still waiting for me." I shook Janine's hand, thanked her for her hospitality, and smiled at her adorable son. As I reached for the door, she invited me to come back anytime, and we could even have tea. Wow, I made a new friend! A song we sang as children came to mind, *"Make new friends but keep the old, one is silver and the other gold."* (*Canciones de Nuestra Cabana,* World Association of Girl Guides and Girl Scouts, 1980).

That night, as I dozed off to sleep, I thanked God for the special gift of wonderful memories. It was great to go back in time, but there was something missing; that was some of the people in the passing of my dad, grandparents, and family pets. It was then I prayed and said to God, *"If possible would You please tell all those family members I love them and still think about them."* I was left with another amazing memory that would always remain with me, along with gratitude for the gentle nudge my friend, Irene, gave me to make it all possible. And to think it all started with a prayer.

"Oil and perfume rejoice the heart; so does the sweetness of a friend's counsel that comes from the heart" (Proverbs 27:9, AMPC).

12

LIFE SAVERS

It started out as just another regular day at work until an act of kindness created peace without a word spoken and in utter silence.

There are many things in life that will catch your eye, but faith helps us see not with our eyes but with our hearts. Life's challenges, although not said out loud, can be seen in the eyes and expressions of others. My co-workers were not yet aware of what we were experiencing, but I guess my aching heart was written on my face. We weren't trying to keep our situation a secret; I just had not emotionally digested what was happening, let alone say it out loud.

A kind person noticed someone with a deep, sad expression and did something extraordinary. Kathy didn't just walk by, but in her caring and respectful way, knew not to ask questions of a broken-hearted friend and possibly pry, but merely gave a gift in silence. A bag of *Life Savers*.

I was the recipient and said, "Thank you," as I graciously accepted the gift. I brought the bag of candy home and stared at it for quite some time, appreciating the candy's actual meaning and so grateful for the beautiful way my friend showed she cared. Sometimes our situations can't change, but we can change the way we react to them, especially after a kind moment. My spirits soured and, in spite of the heart-wrenching pain, I smiled because of the *Life Savers*.

One day there was a sad expression in a co-worker's eyes. I remembered the gracious gift I received and wanted to *pay it forward*, so I brought in a bag of *Life Savers* to give to her. The same lady who initiated this *'gift that keeps on giving'* accepted it with a smile that would soon melt the *Hershey Hugs and Kisses* chocolate I had added to the gift. We laughed and enjoyed the moment and the delicious treats together.

We were taken out of our reverie when a co-worker made a humorous comment that reminded us it was time to go back to work. The moment was over, soon to become a special memory for life. We went back to work a little wiser, soon to discover that the *gift that keeps on giving* might save a life emotionally and, surprisingly, physically.

Soon I couldn't help but noticed a customer who looked to be in distress. I approached her and asked if she needed some assistance. With a weak voice, she said she had forgotten the time and missed an important snack. This could be very serious to a diabetic, and she needed candy to raise her blood sugar level. Before I left to retrieve a candy for her, I made sure she was seated safely on a chair to rest. I asked, "Would you like a chocolate or a *Life Saver* candy?"

She stared at me for a brief moment, thinking about her choices, and said, "A *Life Saver*, please."

I ran to find my friend and quickly explained the emergency, that we had a customer in distress. "She has low blood sugar and is in need of a piece of candy." She quickly opened the bag and pulled out three *Life Savers*—cherry, orange, and lime. I thanked her and began to leave.

"Wait," she said, "there are four flavors, and we forgot the lemon."

I smiled and reached for the last of the four flavors. "Let's give her a chocolate *Hugs and Kisses*, too. I made a dash with the candy for the lady.

In my hurry, I tripped and stubbed my toe, and was just about to shout out in pain when I realized there were people all around. One of the customers saw what I had done, but she never said a word, just smiled as if she were trying not to laugh. I just nodded and smiled back. I kept the pain to myself, quietly, and thought, *you are on the Health and Safety Committee, slow down before there are two of us down and we both need help.* After the slapstick comedy was over, I continued on my mission.

I approached the customer and held out the four flavors. Surprisingly, she chose the lemon, the one we almost forgot. She said that of all the four flavors, lemon was her favorite and she popped it in her mouth with a very shaky hand. After a rest, a refreshing drink of water, and a couple of *Life Savers*, she recovered nicely, but before she left, I handed her a chocolate *Hershey Hugs and Kisses*. She got the humor right away, smiled, and went on her way. I never saw the customer again, but I will always remember the moment.

It was time to get back to the hustle and bustle of the day, but I needed to find my friend to thank her for her quick action and let her know the customer recovered well. With a bright smile, she replied, "Wow! Those truly are *Life Savers*!"

13
WATCH THE BIRDS

The porch swing was rusty and in need of replacement. I began to reminisce about the many warm summer evenings our family enjoyed on that old swing. We read books, checked out cooking recipes, and shared accounts of our daily activities. What I treasured most were the comical stories and laughter Tony and I shared.

Because of so many other financial needs pending, the swing was a luxury at this point, yet a *must-have* that was high on the priority list.

Recently, Tony had been developing new symptoms which indicated his disease was progressing. It was a medical condition called *'ascites'*, a secondary phase of the disease that often appears in the last stages of most chronic illnesses. It caused his abdomen to distend and his ankles to sometimes swell. To relieve the discomfort there was a procedure called *'paracentesis'* to drain the fluid from the patient's abdomen. After this was done, the next day he was always fatigued, and yet grateful to have relief from the pressure.

Sometimes the fluid would become infected, which was serious. We hoped a round of antibiotics would sustain him as he waited for a new organ. Since it was my responsibility to notice any unusual symptoms, it was a blessing to have a direct line to the transplant clinic for directions. I could call at any time, day or night, with our concern, so thankful for the support we received. They mentioned his condition would only worsen as time went on, and they would do their best to give him comfort and relief.

Many times, I thought we were already at the threshold of *worse,* and I would fight back the tears at the thought of my beloved husband experiencing more discomfort. Sometimes the pain in my heart was so great I would rock back and forth to comfort myself, with the reminder there was still hope. Hope was the key that would help keep my chin up, get up, dust myself off, and move forward for the sake of us both.

As Tony and I came closer to the end of our jobs, everything seemed to break down or need replacement, such as the porch swing. Although money was going to be tight, I decided this was important and worth it to splurge. Remembering I was blessed with a new place of employment, with no time to waste, I was on this project immediately. At a local store, I found a beautiful porch swing on sale for half price. Happily, I brought home the box of the unassembled swing. In the past, Tony usually took on these chores, but, as circumstances had changed, so must I change. In the past, I often remarked that we really should learn each other's responsibilities. So now was as good a time as any.

I managed to get the immense, awkward box onto our deck and carefully spread the pieces out in order. It reminded me of a jigsaw puzzle. The job was time-consuming. Focusing on the directions and assembling the project totally took my mind off our current situation. I was relieved and pleased with how smoothly the chore was completed. I checked my handiwork one more time and felt satisfied with my achievement. For a splash of color to create a cheery atmosphere, I also purchased a few throw pillows.

After arranging the rest of the outdoor furniture, I decided to test the safety of my accomplishment. I hopped up on the swing with my friend Gideon, nuzzled close to me. He looked as though he was smiling and content when he licked my cheek in approval. I snuggled him closer and kissed him on the snout. The swing was nice, and I realized the pit of my stomach did not feel as though I was being dropped from a roller coaster, a sensation I often felt.

While I was relaxing, I noticed my devotional book nearby, so I picked it up. The message for the day was about watching the birds. How fascinating. It was from Mathew 6:26-27 (NIV), *"Look at the birds of the air; they do not sow or reap or store away in barns, and yet your heavenly Father feeds them. Are you not much more valuable than they? Can any one of you by worrying add a single hour to your life?"* That verse reminded me of the many occasions Tony would remind me we might have some financial challenges ahead. Although that was an almost constant worry of his, it was not one of mine. My worries were concerning his current and future medical issues only.

Meanwhile, I delighted in hearing the birds cheerfully chirping and singing in the background on this lovely day. As I watched the birds' routine, I began to give my worries to God and trust He would lead us in the right direction and provide for us. Shrugging off the worries, I continued to read and thought *how appropriate to be reading these verses at this exact time in our lives.* A welcome sense of peace seemed to flow through my veins as I read on, eager for guidance.

Then I read verse 34 of Matthew chapter 6 (NIV), *"Therefore do not worry about tomorrow, for tomorrow will worry about itself. Each day has enough trouble of its own."*

Wow, I thought, *the pathway to peace, not anxiety.* Then I heard myself recite that phrase out loud. Suddenly the sound of the birds became very loud and distracting; even Gideon looked up at me, puzzled. I put down my Bible and felt something flutter and slightly graze my cheek. It was a baby bird trying to get my attention. I thought *that was close and startling to say the least.* The verses about watching the birds took on a whole new meaning.

The chirping became even louder, almost like scolding, so I looked in the direction of the commotion as the parents come into view. They were perched on our fence along with their brood and right by the feeder—it was empty. Even though they watched while I filled the feeder every day, they were still cautious of humans. Although the parents were patient about waiting for their meal, the adorable chick was quite eager. A gentle awareness was all it took. Gideon and I climbed off of the swing; our reprieve was over. He yawned, found another cozy spot, and went right back to sleep. Quickly, I went to work filling the feeders.

After the birds' bellies were full, I climbed back up on our new swing, this time sprawled out with my head on the comfy new throw pillows. There it was again, that all-too-familiar feeling in the pit of my stomach. I realized why assembling the swing was important to me; Tony would soon be home after another round in the hospital. He had been there for three days and his condition was improving, temporarily. It was necessary to have a cozy area outdoors for him to enjoy the fresh air as we waited for his eventual return to good health.

After a bit of rest, with a conscious effort not to worry and make myself sick, I took a moment to think about all our blessings; there were so many. When I got my emotions in check, I went inside and fed Gideon an early dinner. I didn't have much of an appetite, yet I still made it a point to eat properly. I made a julienne salad with ham, cheese, turkey, and several vegetables. The meal was really tasty, and I soon started to feel a bit stronger from some necessary nutrition, physically and spiritually.

I let Gideon outside one more time. While I waited for him, I took a moment to look in the mirror, only to see a disheveled mess. I brushed my hair, washed my face, and applied a little makeup, hoping to appear cheerful, because seeing Tony at the hospital was painful for me. I believed if I cleaned up nicely and looked my best, it would be encouraging and lift his spirits. When he saw my raw emotions, it made him feel bad. He had enough to contend with without dealing with my emotions, too.

One day, he caught me crying alone, and when he asked what was wrong, I only cried all the more because I didn't want him to see me at my breaking point. When I got myself together, I said, honestly, "I am in severe emotional pain over our situation, and I want to tell my best friend about how I feel; only my best friend is you." I continued, "I am trying to be strong for both of us and today I cannot. I feel completely broken."

I will never forget the sorrow on his face when he said, "From this point on, we are in this together; always tell me how you are feeling." He was giving me permission to be myself and continue sharing with him as we always had.

I decided to take my furry son, Gideon, along for the ride to the hospital so he could stretch his legs and work his magic. He was a trained therapy dog and was allowed to enter most public buildings and hospitals. I clothed him in his working garb and snuggled him one more time as we left the house for the hospital to be with Tony as he ate his dinner. I was so grateful this time the hospital was local and very convenient. I decided not to pay for parking as we were watching our funds, so parking on the street became a good source of exercise for me.

Before walking toward the hospital, I looked into the sky which was darkening as if a storm was brewing, *I should eventually go to the dollar store and buy an umbrella to keep in the glove compartment, just in case.* I opened the door too quickly and it swung back, slightly crushing my foot. I was annoyed and tired of getting hurt in the rush. Gideon just appeared to be smiling, as if he enjoyed the comedy. I exited the car quickly, hoping to get inside before the storm started. Reminding myself not to run and get hurt even more, I walked at a steady pace, with Gideon leading the way, and made it inside the hospital just in time, safely.

For a moment we watched the sky burst into an amazing rainstorm. I always enjoy the wonder of it, while sheltered. Gideon had special training, so he never cowered during thunder or rain storms. As we walked down the hall of the emergency area, a young lad came into view and Gideon tugged on his leach to halt. The boy and his parents looked distraught with their heads down in sadness. When they noticed Gideon, suddenly they started to smile as if taking a vacation from their current situation. I explained who we were and asked if it was okay for Gideon, our therapy dog, to visit.

With excitement, Gideon went to work immediately. He was a therapy dog for the mending of heart and soul. I was always amazed as I watched him work his magic. My job was to hold his leash while he did all the work. He was friendly, and charming, and lived up to his name, Gideon. It was a privilege to be a part of his special ministry. The name *Gideon* always sparked an interest in a Bible story from the book of Judges, to which I was happy to relate.

I noticed something was wrong with the boy's ankle, and before I spoke, the parents mentioned that during a pre-championship hockey game, he was injured. It was the last game of the playoffs and, if the team won, it would bring them to the championship. I well remember when our son played hockey and Tony coached. It was heartwarming to see the pride in both parents' eyes. I could relate because we were always proud of our son or daughter when they played sports.

As the young lad was pleasantly distracted by Gideon, the parents said they were waiting for the x-ray results and hopefully his ankle was not broken. I noticed it was getting late and I didn't want to miss keeping Tony company while he ate his dinner. We said our goodbyes and started to leave. Gideon, once again, put on the brakes and went back to the room to comfort the boy one more time. Hearts melted with a tear in every eye. Gideon had done the work of a saint and I was proud of him.

Together we walked through the emergency area and down a long hallway to an elevator that took us to Tony's room. My heart sank when he came into view. His colour was noticeably grey, and he looked sad. As I spoke, he seemed to perk up and be happy to see me and surprised to see his furry son, Gideon. I sat by his bedside. After showing his daddy some attention, Gideon rested at the end of the bed. Soon the dinner tray arrived. Nutrition was very important to keep up his strength for the hope of an upcoming surgery.

Sadly, he had very little appetite, so as his helper, I mindlessly began to feed him. Too weak to object, he would open his mouth. To get our minds off our current situation, I asked, "At this point in time what is important to you?"

He knew the answer immediately; with a weak smile he answered, "My wish is to be home with you and our family for holidays and birthdays."

"That is a really nice wish," I said.

He continued, "I want to be able to walk our daughter down the aisle when she gets married soon." My heart broke, but I hid the tears. That was one of my requests in my daily prayers, too.

When the meal was finished, Tony fell fast asleep. I moved from the side of the bed to a chair and watched him sleep. He lost the peaceful look he had when he was well. We often referred to these moments as our own personal '*Titanic*,' referring to the part where the boat sank and they were all floating on lifeboats when one of the characters said, *"Basically we are waiting to live or waiting to die."* Also, there was the fact there weren't enough lifeboats for everyone who was on board. It was a reminder there might not be an organ available for him or many other patients who were waiting—a thought that often crushed me and pained my heart.

I prayed and asked God if it were possible to have a *lifeboat* for Tony and to rescue us both from this painful, agonizing time we were enduring. I remembered the scripture verses I read earlier about *Watch the Birds*. While Tony slept, I asked God to show me a way not to worry so much and relax my aching soul in His care. Suddenly the memory of watching the bird family brought comfort. Now my soul was basking in God's peace. I looked up and winked, and thanked Him for answering my prayer so quickly. I glanced out the window; the storm had stopped and I was treated to a rainbow.

I felt showered with many blessings lately, even as we dealt with the struggles of anxiety and the worry of waiting. I knew the precious gifts God gave me were not to keep for myself but to be shared with Tony and others along the way. I whispered, *"I entrust our situation to You, Lord."* I patted Gideon on the head and sat back in my chair.

I realized that when we find ourselves fidgeting and frustrated, we have to stop and simply *wait*, whether at a checkout line, waiting for results after a job interview, dealing with car repairs, etc. It was like being temporarily put on hold. All these situations paled against the intensity of waiting for medical tests or going on a list for a new organ. I looked at my husband with tears streaming down my cheeks and thought *I can only imagine how you feel*. I kissed his forehead and whispered, "I love you."

> *"Don't worry about anything; instead, pray about everything. Tell God what you need, and thank Him for all He has done. Then*

you will experience God's peace, which exceeds anything we can understand. His peace will guard your hearts and minds as you live in Christ Jesus" (Philippians 4:6-7, NLT)

14

One Small Pin and One Giant Leap of Faith

While reading recipes, my thoughts were interrupted, by the reminder of a very important turning point in my life. I had just agreed to speak publicly for the first time, on behalf of a counselling centre, about the results of marriage counselling and the gift of freedom when they helped me overcome anxiety. When receiving these valuable gifts, they are meant to be shared with others so they, too, will know there is hope.

Just when I thought I had leaped over enough stumbling blocks of fears and phobias, I was now going to face the biggest one of all—public speaking. Even the thought caused the anxiety to become more intense. In addition, I discovered I was going to be centered out at work. It all began with one small pin (an award) I was to receive.

It reminded me of when Neal Armstrong stepped on the moon for the first time and proclaimed, *"One small step for man and one giant leap for mankind."* I had no intentions of flying to the moon, but the fear was as scary as the thought of being in closed quarters in a rocket, leaping out of a plane, or falling backward while roped to a mountain. Public speaking should pale to all of those challenges, but it didn't. There was a giant knot in my stomach that terrified me.

While enjoying the daily routine of work, the manager made an announcement over the loudspeaker calling all employees to a staff meeting. On the way, I overheard it was regarding a staff member who would receive an award. When I realized they were calling this meeting to thank me for an achievement, I became paralyzed with fear, grabbed my coat, and left. The fact my shift was over covered my tracks, but only temporarily. This was getting ridiculous. Fear of speaking in front of a group was interfering with too many areas of my life, and now to the point where I couldn't even accept an award in front of my co-workers.

I rushed home and closed the door behind me; for a brief moment, I felt safe. However, remorse set in, and I gained the courage to confess. I picked up the phone and, without hesitation, called the manager. It took a moment for her to answer because the line was constantly busy, and now I was interrupting her day with my discomfort. She had already been informed it was me, because even before I spoke, she said, "You missed your award! I heard you left for the day. No worries, we will just do it tomorrow."

Tomorrow! I thought I had already escaped.

I knew it was time to confess, "About that, I left on purpose because I am terrified to be singled out in public, even for a good reason. I am painfully shy about speaking to a group."

There was an unsettling silence for a moment. Finally, she spoke. "I can understand that for some people, but not you." Her impression of me was that I appeared confident and generally outgoing which didn't help my cause. Even though I became a master at escape, it was not going to work this time. It appeared her mind was made up and she was not going to take no for an answer. I gave it a good try, even though I was already defeated.

I mentioned that in the past when I knew it was time to receive an award, I would briefly explain my situation to previous managers who would simply hand over the award with no questions asked. Relief would come over me until the next time. That strategy worked well until today because she was a new manager. I continued to explain, expecting the same results as always, and I would go back to my comfortable world. Only that was not what happened; she challenged me instead. Her reply was, "It is important for you to receive an award in front of co-workers because it gives them an incentive and encourages others." She was very kind in her decision, and I appreciated her encouragement.

I thanked her for caring and there was a sort of trust when I agreed to receive the award publicly. I cringed at the thought and wondered *what is with me lately being so agreeable to face more fears?* When the conversation was over, I hung up the phone. Tony overheard what was said, saw my expression was not good and was naturally concerned. "What is wrong with you?"

I explained briefly and he got the whole picture; *he knows me well.*

I love the way Tony can turn any situation into a comedy. He suddenly appeared forlorn and walked to the window with his head down and a sad look on his face. I said, jokingly, "Now what is wrong with *you?*"

"Well," he said, "I don't want to go to work tomorrow because someone might try to thank me."

I smiled. "Are you mocking me?" We both laughed over how ridiculous the situation had become.

Through the silliness, I conceded, "I get the point."

He continued, "You are not going to work to get a public spanking; you are going for a public thanking." Then I laughed until tears streamed down my cheeks—*tears of joy.*

However, the next day was not so funny. I was terrified all day, and for nothing, because we were much too busy at work to acknowledge me. Every day that followed I would think *what if this is the day they thank me,* and feel sick. I couldn't quit my job over a *thank you.* Doesn't that sound silly? The day finally came. I heard the manager call a meeting over the loudspeaker and I knew this was it. My first reaction was to run away as I had always done in the past. Only this time something was different; I knew I couldn't leave. I began to pray, *please help me get through this moment.* It was just one small pin.

I noticed our manager had no problem speaking publicly; she appeared poised and confident. I thought *I could learn from her.* Suddenly, I began to shake from head to toe, knees knocking, and the discomfort was unbearable. The manager handled the situation beautifully. The process was so simple. She did all the speaking and soon I heard a very shaky voice I hardly recognized, say, "Thank you." When it was all over, I realized my worries were a complete waste of time.

Everyone went back to work, except Sandie, the manager, and Silvana, our human resources person; they stayed behind to have a chat. Both knew about my fear and really cared. During our conversation, I mentioned I was invited to share publicly a story of overcoming fear and about the support the Centre had given our family during several crises. They were not surprised as I had already mentioned briefly some of the challenges we were facing. They looked at each other, then looked back at me and smiled. "We think that is a great idea. You have to do it and keep us posted."

I confessed, in the past, I had missed too many opportunities. I will never forget the help and support I received. As she said, "We understand," the manager told a story about not being *'a wallflower.'* I was so grateful for our management team and continued to learn from two ladies who were definitely not *wallflowers*. I thanked them for their encouragement. Eventually, their kind words led, not only to more courage but to many other challenges and opportunities.

Suddenly I was awakened from the reverie to hear my name being called by my counsellor. "Hi, Debbie, I am sorry, I'm running late." She greeted me with a big smile and a gentle hug. I was so grateful for her and, through time, she became a good friend.

I thanked God for placing these wonderful women in my life and for the gifts they shared with me which I wanted to pass on, hoping to help others, even if it meant overcoming yet another fear.

"Kind words are like honey—sweet to the soul and healthy for the body" (Proverbs 16:24, NLT). Little did I know that by simply saying *yes*, it would lead to overcoming many more fears, and eventually gaining strength and confidence for what giant steps we were going to face in the future. Not only was I *in training* for what was to come, but I became a stronger *me*. And to think it all began with one small pin and one giant leap of faith.

15
Don't Go It Alone

For almost twenty years we frequented a hospital some distance away. The days were very long, involving procedures and tests. Waiting for Tony gave me time with other caregivers while they waited as well. After listening to their stories, I would often ask, "What is your support system?" The answers varied, but the outcome was similar: friends, family, food, or wine. Then I asked, "How is that working for you?"

All had the same answer, "Not very well. Although family and friends can be helpful, we don't want to be a burden to others."

We were on a friendly basis, so I continued, "Did you ever consider outside help."

Most of the answers were, "We can go it alone." Next, they would ask, "How about you?"

My answer to my own question was . . .

While waiting at the Centre for caregiving support, I picked up a magazine with a picture of delicious food on the cover. I couldn't wait to see the recipes, so I turned the pages enthusiastically. Unexpectedly, I felt a cozy sense of peace flow through me. I had often heard that that feeling may occur when others are praying for us. I bookmarked a recipe that caught my eye and set the magazine on my lap to bask in the peace.

I felt comfort in knowing I had come to the right place for support and even their brochure photo sported a rainbow over the top of the

Centre which was not planned when the photo was taken. As I glanced around the waiting area; my eyes settled on the front door. I thought about my first visit many years ago when we came here for marriage counselling. Yes, marriage counselling, and what a gift we received.

Just crossing the threshold was not easy. I understood the term *we can go it alone* because I believed it. Secretly I had called several hotlines looking for advice; the response was great—a stranger to listen to our story. As comforting as they were, I needed to find help locally. That first day, with a shaky hand on the knob of the front door, I actually looked over both shoulders to make sure no one noticed me enter the building. My life was challenging at the moment, and I didn't have the energy to explain to others all we were dealing with. And my confidence level was floundering as well.

Denial finally erupted in our faces. Denial is a normal *getaway*, emotionally, before accepting the reality of one's situation. We were both in that *'comfy phase'* for several years; then the next stage of emotions hit us. It came on suddenly like *'a thief in the night.'* As job loss and the fear of transplant drew nearer, anger set in. We needed to love each other more, not less, during difficult times, but at that point, it was not easy.

From what was explained to me, there are five stages of grief: denial, anger, bargaining, depression, and then acceptance. Each can surface at different times and can come back again.

Waiting for answers to more medical tests, and job loss for both of us added to Tony's frustration.

I struggled to keep peace and harmony in spite of everything. We finally realized that during all the shouting matches, we were not really hearing each other over the escalation of noise; we were just venting. Sadly, there were no solutions or answers because this situation was new to us. Enough was enough. I knew our problems were much bigger than we could handle.

My goal was to get back to the life to which we were accustomed. Then I prayed, *is it possible to get to an even better place?*

Initially, when I mentioned outside help, Tony took offense and refused to go. He actually believed we could get through the disarray and confusion on our own, but I knew better. Out of love for my family,

I called for outside help. It was not some sort of admission of defeat or weakness, but a commitment to regaining strength and order in our home so we would be prepared for the *worse* to come.

I glanced around the Centre and recalled a day something wonderful had happened right here in this building. I came looking for answers, and I received even more than I asked for. The miracle started when Tony noticed the positive changes in me. Prayer was answered when, eventually, he joined me for counselling. The breaking point was the mere thought that I wanted to leave my marriage, not because of the long haul of caregiving, but my heart kept breaking from all the strife. I developed chest pains that became so strong I finally had to have them checked out.

After a series of tests, it appeared a condition was starting to take root, which would only get worse if I declined to manage it. It was revealed in the statement *"stress can kill us."* A thought popped into my mind: *the caregiver can end up in worse shape than the patient.* The prognosis was: this is a fair warning and a gift at the same time. With the knowledge of how to manage your stress, you can totally reverse your current medical condition. Make sure you eat a healthy diet and exercise. There would never be a lack of stress, so I decided to certainly do my best.

Through several months of counselling, we stopped struggling and the unnecessary bickering subsided. No matter what we were currently facing or going to face, we would do it together—for life. God and our prayers became bigger than any problem. Our love grew as we moved on with new hope for the future, hand in hand. Although we had many challenges ahead of us, these became stepping stones to a calmer, more peaceful end. We both became more disciplined with a better measure of self-control.

Once our marriage became secure, it was time to deal with other issues. When it was revealed I suffered from a lifetime of anxiety, the counsellors encouraged me by sharing that many others were healed of the same thing. And to think I had convinced myself I would be plagued with this disorder for life. Healing began. Anxiety proved to be much smaller than anything else I had to deal with in my life. I now had a trust in God and a Christ-infused confidence; others noticed and commented, *"You have become so strong I hardly recognize you."*

I was honest, "It is not me; it is my relationship with our Maker."

I have to confess—it took a lot of hard work, including homework. The homework was every bit as important as the appointments with a counsellor. Although stress was a part of life, by putting God first, my anxiety gradually decreased, and I became a new, more refreshed person.

Soon I was invited to share our success stories with tours at the Centre. For the longest time, I said no. I was not comfortable sharing our personal story, especially in front of a group of people because I was terrified of public speaking. Also, I was taught that you keep your personal business within your own four walls.

One day after a counselling session, I was so grateful for the healing I received, that when I was invited again to speak publicly, I agreed. I wanted to share the help we received with the hope of helping others. I heard myself say, "Yes."

I remember kicking myself all the way home. Not only did I have a sickening fear of public speaking but had to write my own material; I knew I was neither a writer nor a speaker. Just when I thought my anxiety was healed, the whole week leading up to the big day was much bigger in my mind than it should actually have been.

I talk to people every day, so I asked myself, *"What is the fear?"* It became obvious—I didn't want to feel judged, and I was concerned about what people thought of me. Standing in front of any group no matter how large or small, caused crippling fear. Just introducing myself and saying my name in a group caused the jitters. I did everything I could to hide this emotion and hoped no one noticed. I had just said *yes* to face one of my biggest fears. So, I mustered up the courage and thought *I can do this.*

After the drive home, I took the *'plunge'* and began a study on overcoming the fear of public speaking. I remembered the story of Moses and his fear when asked to speak on behalf of God. Although I knew the story, I never applied it to my current situation until I read it again. With God's help, Moses was able to speak publicly and that inspired me to continue. I would do it despite my fear, with God's help.

I reminded myself of 2 Timothy 1:7 (NLT), *"For God has not given us a spirit of fear and timidity, but of power, love, and self discipline."* Looking up, I asked for *some of that, please.*

I was awakened from my reverie when the receptionist mentioned it would be just a few more minutes. I smiled and said, "Thank you!" I picked up my magazine and continued to check out recipes until I was called for my session. I enjoyed the quiet peace and was thankful for a place where you don't have to *'go it alone.'*

16
Listen to Learn and Learn to Listen

If you rearrange the letters in the word *"listen,"* the word *"silent"* can be formed from the exact same letters. Pastor Bob shared that during one of his sermons. Throughout the message, he pointed out the importance of the word *"listen."* He also talked about how listening and silence obviously go together. This message spoke loud and clear to many in the congregation that day. It challenged us to become better listeners, more focused, and truly care about what was being said to us.

During tours at the Centre, I noticed one of the key phrases was, *listen to learn.* After gaining a better grasp on controlling anxiety, I also gained the ability to listen better. It is sometimes difficult to hear or concentrate when one's mind is consumed with worry. As I became a quieter version of myself by *listening,* my comprehension developed. At the time, several people mentioned that is why God gave us two ears and one mouth. In other words, we must listen more and speak less.

Those messages became important stepping stones. Tony developed what appeared to be some very uncomfortable symptoms and, even though he claimed he was alright, his facial expressions gave him away. I asked him to describe his symptoms, remembering it is very important to listen carefully, keep silent while listening, and gather all the facts in order to explain his symptoms to his doctors.

Gradually it became more difficult for Tony to share symptoms verbally. Because he did not want to go back to the hospital, he would try to hide how he felt. It was then the assessments went to a whole new level. I began to quietly examine his facial expressions: his eyes and his color, without words, in silence. The mere mention it was time to go to the hospital would cause him anxiety; he would become frustrated and appear angry. Quite simply, he just needed my patience, understanding, and support. My emotions were not as easy as flipping a light switch, so I asked God to tame the emotions of us both.

When the distressing announcement was inevitable—time to go to the hospital—I would calmly soften my voice. Then I would slip out of our room to give him some space for a moment so he could adjust to this shattering news. I quickly got things ready, so he wouldn't become sidetracked by the appearance of my tears. If I stayed in the room with him, he would expect an argument, but I knew we both needed our strength and energy for what was to come.

Even though doctors mentioned his hospital visits would become more frequent, preparing one's sensitivity for those days and many more to come was challenging for me. I prayed for composure as I ushered my husband out into the night. My goal was to get medical attention as soon as possible to relieve his distress and any discomfort. As I drove him to the hospital, I reminded myself to focus, because it was often late when his new symptoms occurred. Sometimes I was on my last nerve during these times and had to remind myself no matter how tired and weary I was, he was much worse.

One time, as we were driving down our street, Tony became enraged and started to beat up the dashboard, one fist at a time. Where he got the energy and strength to do this was a mystery to me. He hit the dashboard so hard so many times I thought the airbag was going to deploy. I often wondered why, in the past, when I would try to stifle this behavior, it only made matters worse. What made the difference this time was, I put God and Tony first and not the peace I was so badly striving for. It was about submitting to *slow to speak, quick to listen, slow to anger* I had been studying about.

I pulled the car over. "I don't know how it feels to be you, and you don't really know what it's like to be me in these circumstances. The truth is, if I were you, maybe I would beat up the car, too. When you are through taking your emotions out on the car, I will continue driving."

He threw a few more punches to get it out of his system, then, calmly said, "I am ready to go." This was a turning point for both of us, and we stepped over yet another threshold as a loving couple.

To lighten the moment, I shared a story from the past. During our first year of marriage, I was so upset one day, I punched the wall and to my surprise, my hand went right through. It took his mind off the present moment, and he said, "Oh yeah, I remember the time, and it took me a few hours to fix the drywall."

"Often you have been my saving grace."

The moment was over abruptly when he made a few groaning noises and his face showed signs of pain. I reached over and squeezed his knee. "I love you."

"I love you, too."

I said, "When I called the doctor to report your symptoms, he confirmed the necessity to bring you in right away, tonight, and he would meet us there."

He changed the subject. "You know the kids' weddings are coming up and I need to be healthy enough so I can walk our daughter down the aisle." Silence overcame us. I hoped he did not see the tears streaming down my cheeks. I prayed he would have his wish and continued to drive in the darkness of the night. I was grateful our local hospital was so close to home.

I walked him inside and when he was safe, I parked the car. The walk and fresh air helped compose a frazzled version of myself. I entered the hospital and as I wandered down the hall there it was again, in the pit of my stomach, the feeling like I was being dropped from the first giant hill on a roller coaster. I joined Tony and sat beside him.

When our family doctor arrived, I could see we had interrupted his rest, too. I said, "Tony didn't think his symptoms were bad enough and wanted to wait till the morning, but I didn't want to second guess who was right, so that is why I called you."

After several tests, the doctor actually thanked me for bringing him to the hospital. His test results proved to be serious, but with proper rest and medication, he would be alright. Relief came over me.

To the doctor, I said, "By the way, Tony mentioned a concern. Our children are getting married soon and he is worried his health will not permit him to walk our daughter down the aisle."

He replied, "We will do our best."

After all the commotion settled, we both thanked the doctor as he left to go home. He looked exhausted and in need of a good night's rest. I often prayed for him.

I stayed with Tony until he fell asleep, then went home with a heavy heart.

At the workplace, I talked as little as possible about our situation, because at this point everything was still manageable.

The doors finally closed at the job I loved for so many years. With God's help, I moved forward to a new adventure. It was imperative to get a proper rest because my new job required me to get an early start and be quick on my feet.

"Listen to learn" became very important—both at home and at work. There were so many new challenges and new fears to be conquered. The advice I had heard about fear from others was: *'don't run, learn to face it.'* When that feeling tried to invade my soul and I wanted to bolt, I simply asked God to keep my feet even more firmly grounded. The key word that should accompany *listening* was *"Love."* If we love someone, we will want to listen to them and hope they will listen to us. Love for each other becomes even more important when the situations are far from lovely.

17

BUSY OR BALANCED

I have always loved serving people and taking a moment to listen to the stories of the people in our town. In the midst of small talk, one question often arose, "Dear, are you keeping busy?"

In the past my answer was mindlessly the same, "Oh yeah, keeping busy." However, the depth of this once effortless answer had changed; my life seemed to be bursting at the seams with an overflow of '*busy.*'

This innocent question began to sting and should have been an indication that, through over-busyness, burnout was beginning to fester. With no let-up, life was catching up with me. I totally missed the warning signs, such as fatigue, sadness, and a general loss of joy. Foolishly I continued to believe I was a tower of strength and unbreakable.

Caregiving along with other obligations and responsibilities seemed to be colliding and the weight of an over-busy life was getting too heavy. My emotions finally erupted. I was alone in an empty room sitting on the floor, hiding from the world, not wanting to be found out. As I cried about many things, it occurred to me there was a fine line between busy and balanced.

Tony's health continued to decline, and we were getting closer to the moment of truth. Would his health hold out for our son's wedding in August and our daughter's wedding in October? Within five months there were six events scheduled: two bridal showers, two 'stag and does,' and two weddings.

Our family was relieved Tony's health was stable enough to make it through the first four events. Although he was fatigued most of the time, he was not in any pain. We were so grateful and hoped it would continue for the two most important events— the weddings.

It wasn't long before Tony developed new symptoms. Through many tests, the doctors confirmed he was now in *stage four* of his illness. Once again, the symptoms were greater than the care I could give him at home, so hospitalization was required. Each time he was hospitalized was another steppingstone of hope he would soon receive his transplant and *he would get better.*

During a moment when we were alone, Tony mustered up enough energy to share his concerns. As he glanced around the hospital room, he became completely transparent. "What if I can't make it to the weddings?"

A chill came over me as I sat very still and just listened. Sadly, he mentioned backup just in case he wasn't able, for some reason, to walk our daughter down the aisle.

That comment caused an intense struggle to stop my tears from flowing. Our family was aware that might happen, so arrangements had already been made. Our daughter asked her new father-in-law-to-be to step in, if necessary, and he was honored to help.

I excused myself and quickly left the room before the flood began. Even though he gave me permission to share my feelings, I couldn't bear the pain in Tony's eyes as he watched me crumble. I bolted to the palliative care family room, which most hospitals have for the families of chronic or terminally ill patients. The solitude of this cozy room had become my friend. I appreciated the comfy sofa that was often my place of letting it all out. To my surprise, the room was already occupied by another family, so I excused myself and went outside for some fresh air instead.

As the tears stained my face with an unstoppable force, my thoughts went to the fact that lately, his days at work had become more challenging. Each day the inevitable became clearer—it would soon be time for him to stop working. We were pleasantly surprised and relieved he had been able to attend both 'stags and does' and two bridal showers without interruption. We thanked God for making that possible. That thought gave me the courage to continue and I returned to my husband's bedside.

As I wandered the hospital hallways, images of the visible changes in him came to mind. Although family and friends noticed and commented on his physical appearance, I was grateful they were polite by not dwelling on the situation. Everyone seemed to understand the wonder and excitement of these special events for our family. We were enjoying a reprieve from his current medical situation.

On my way back to Tony's room, I paused at the maternity ward for a moment. Both our daughter and son were born right here in this hospital, with Tony by my side for support during the pains of natural childbirth. It seemed like yesterday; now they were both adults getting ready to start a new chapter of their own lives. A pleasant thought crossed my mind and caused my heart to melt. It was the hope Tony and I would have grandchildren one day. I prayed Tony would be with us and healthy for those precious days to come.

I stopped for a moment to freshen up, and while looking in the mirror, it occurred to me the years were starting to catch up with me. I am kind to the aging lady in the mirror and welcome the laugh lines and the jowls now apparent. I applied some color to my face, blush and lipstick in a soft shade of pink. With one last look in the mirror, I reminded myself everything would eventually fall into place and be alright. I was now stable enough to return to Tony. It was no surprise to find him sound asleep. I kissed his forehead and went home.

After a few days in the hospital, Tony was able to return home. We always celebrated his homecoming and continued with his proper diet and rest. He seemed refreshed and there was a sense of normality for a while. Another event loomed on the horizon—our daughter and son-in-law-to-be had signed the papers for their dream home and our daughter was moving out.

While Tony rested, I sat beside him and shared the good news. He was genuinely happy for our daughter but frustrated with his inadequate strength to be able to help with the move. I set his mind at rest when I assured him, we had plenty of help.

When moving day arrived, he felt he had enough strength to help with the smaller things. He appeared happy and content to be a part of this special day.

After we had finished moving the last of her belongings into the truck and it was time to go, my emotions got the best of me. There is a term for this day—the *"empty nest syndrome."* Since I had become so grounded by praying, the busyness of this day became less painful as I gave all my pain to God, which seemed natural—until I saw her empty room!

As sudden, like a bolt of lightning, my emotions began to explode and to think I was doing so well up to this point. It took my breath away. I swiftly waved them on and said, "I will catch up with you soon. Go ahead."

I made it just in time without being found out. The tears of reality started at the thought that my little girl was all grown up. I slumped down in the middle of her empty room and all my emotions erupted into a very loud howl of crying. The thought that my life was going through too many changes all at once, made matters worse. Thinking I was alone, I bellowed even louder.

In my deep sorrow, I never heard the front door open; my solitude had been interrupted and I was in shock. What was worse, my tower of strength crumbled, and I had been found out. Through tear-blurred vision, I saw the concerned faces of my daughter and my husband. I thought they were going to make fun of me, but instead, they sat down on the carpet beside me. With a shaky voice, I said I thought they had already left and I needed a moment. Apparently, my *'getaway'* expression had given me away.

When they heard the sound of my sobbing, they just wanted to console me. Gently, they put their arms around me. They had anticipated this moment would be difficult for me, and my emotional eruption was only a matter of time. Their comfort and care were the best medicine, and to think I thought it was best *to go it alone*. Warmth coursed through my body and I was blessed by their presence.

When my daughter reminded me their dream home was only around the corner within walking distance, we all started to laugh. Humor was one thing that knit us together as a family, especially during tough times. We were grateful our friend *'humour'* always put us back on track. The tears slowed to a few sniffles. Their love and care worked a miracle. I felt much better and had a memory to hold on to forever.

My family's love, encouragement, and kind words refreshed me. I thanked them for their concern. Needing a moment to myself, I told them would be back on track shortly, to which they agreed without questions or comments. When I was completely alone, I thanked God for the tears that washed away my sorrows, and for a loving family who allowed me the freedom to show emotion. I thanked Him for the realization *I don't have to go it alone.*

Although I have read in the Bible that God wants us to depend on Him, sometimes I fall short and need to ask Him to show me how to trust Him more. As I began to count our many blessings, I looked up and winked. From that moment, through prayer in all situations, I changed and became the tower of strength Tony could trust and count on. As I continued to ponder, reality set in. As a caregiver, my life would become even fuller and there would be no let-up as time went by. It was then I felt the need to ask God for the strength of two people, and to teach me to know how to draw the line between busy and balanced.

18
Prayers and Blessings

The day I married Tony was one of the best days of my life until our children were born. They completed our family with what I refer to as *the best days of our lives*. Our daughter and son seem to have matured through 'the express lane' of life and now their wedding days were approaching fast.

Our son landed his dream job and at the same time, he and his lovely wife-to-be bought their dream home, a charming house close to home. Again, I reminded myself *it is only one block away*, just like our daughter's house, both within walking distance.

Since our daughter already paved the way for the empty nest, I was better prepared, emotionally, for when our son moved out. I was elated both children had met their 'perfect match.' We were doubly blessed when they both purchased houses close to home, which kept my emotions at bay. I began to imagine our grandchildren would be just around the corner, too, someday. It was great to be sharing what would be one of many special occasions to come with Stacey's parents, Jim and Mary, a kind, caring, and fun-loving couple.

It was imperative for Tony's health to hold up a little longer for the two weddings, a couple of months apart.

Distressingly, as Tony's health declined, his body changed in appearance. His belly was now distended most of the time and the weight of the fluid retention was very uncomfortable. His ankles often swelled, too, which was expected in the last stages of most illnesses. The diuretic medication helped to prevent water retention for a while, but eventually, it began to insult his kidneys, so he had to stop taking it temporarily. Then the discomfort of heavy weight gain returned. When his blood tests were a bit more stable, he would start a series of diuretics again until he was advised to stop.

Before matters became much worse, it was imperative for Tony to get fitted for his suit for the wedding with, hopefully, no interruptions. His arms and legs at this point were skin and bones with no muscle tone. Before we left the house, he glanced in the mirror and said with shock, "My body looks like *Bullwinkle*!" He was very fatigued from the extra weight, but gallant to even endeavour to go for a fitting.

We drove to Niagara Falls. When I helped him out of the car, he mentioned his belly felt too heavy and the discomfort was worsening. As he walked into the men's wear store, he leaned forward because he was weighed down and my heart sank at the thought of his anguish. It was abundantly clear we needed many prayers to help us through the days ahead.

Those who helped Tony with his fitting were aware there was an underlying condition. The clerks were very respectful and polite and did not to ask too many questions. It was a relief we didn't have to go into details which often took away needed energy. They could see he was very ill, so no words were needed. His color was off and his eyes were sunken. He appeared critical but was a rock to continue.

I began to pray quietly, asking God to please help Tony make it through our son's wedding, and with a measure of comfort, too. I also prayed to have him by my side, as I couldn't bear the thought of an empty space or chair without him. I was grateful he was able to make it through all of the events so far. As I witness his distress, he became my hero, and my love for him grew even greater.

He was such an amazingly good sport throughout each event. I thought *kudos to the counsellors who were helping both of us keep our chins up and were praying for us every day.* As life became more challenging, they committed to helping us through the long haul of his illness. The support of professionals certainly made a difference for us.

Facing the unknown head-on was not easy. I merely adjusted to the fact I would remain in a constant state of emotional pain. The stress over the uncertainty of our future had risen to a new level. However, I had gained better coping skills to help Tony's health hold out for not one, but two weddings so close together. The excitement of the weddings was our main focus, *while we are waiting*.

Meanwhile, the sales clerks did their best to fit Tony, and we thanked them as we left. It was a nice day and, if all went well, I had planned on going out for lunch. I called ahead to make sure the restaurant offered low-sodium food on their menu. It was a blessing most restaurants could accommodate such a request. I was elated when Tony said he would be happy to go out for lunch. Sitting across from each other, I was relieved to see he had an appetite and said he needed this outing. My heart welled up with joy that he was visibly enjoying himself. For just a moment it felt like old like old times. We actually did something *normal*—we went out for lunch.

A few days without diuretics caused Tony's belly to distend even more to the point where it became unbearable. Aware of his condition, doctors mentioned that if there were any changes, to call immediately, which I did. We met our family doctor at urgent care and explained the situation about our son's wedding. He was very sympathetic. He recommended a procedure to remove the fluid and ordered blood work to determine if Tony would be able to start taking the diuretic medication again.

Immediate action was taken to relieve Tony's discomfort—the fluid that was weighing him down physically and emotionally. Our doctor worked with Tony's specialist in Toronto by phone because of the distance. Together they made a wonderful team to keep Tony patched up for the weddings. After the procedure, Tony felt instant relief and was able to come home. As always, we celebrated his return.

All went well until the next day. He developed new symptoms that seemed to affect his thinking. I was concerned his blood sugar levels had dropped because the liver was failing, which could throw his diabetes into a tailspin. The specialist mentioned this could occur, so I asked Tony to check his sugar level. After a few attempts, he appeared very confused, as if he had forgotten how to prick his own finger to draw blood for the meter. Previous training had prepared me for this; when I checked, his levels were perfectly fine.

Since some symptoms may mimic several other conditions, I called the doctor right away, and back to urgent care we went. As it turned out, from the diuretics and the removal of fluid he was dehydrated. We made sure he drank enough water, but in spite of our best efforts, this condition still occurred. He was kept overnight on IVs and, once again, he bounced back. When he came home, he said he felt as good as new. I often wondered when he said that if it was for my benefit not to worry. We made sure he was fully rested every day until the wedding.

The wedding day arrived. Tony was well and energetic. When he tried on his suit, it was a little too big because of removing the belly fluid, and weight he had lost from the procedure. In spite of all he had been through to get to this very special day, he looked exceptionally handsome. I mentioned how good-looking he was and his eyes were glaring at me as if he had not heard that compliment. Then he said I looked as beautiful as on our wedding day. I made a joke, "There is a smooth talker in our house today."

It was no surprise we were blessed with good health for Tony on our son's wedding day because so many people were praying for us. I am sure it was God who helped Tony get through to that day so successfully. I was overjoyed at the thought that God was so good to us, and tears of joy were running down my cheeks in gratitude. Although I had the occasional *stream* of tears, today Tony and I shared *a waterfall* of joy. While Tony finished getting ready, I sat down for a moment to thank God for His many blessings and especially for the prayers He had answered.

19

A Fun Adventure

After checking on Tony, I was elated his health today was stable. He was *definitely* able to attend our son's wedding. For a moment, I glanced at the years of photos scattered across the walls throughout our home. As a tear rolled down my cheek, it was a tear of letting go. My adorable little boy was now a man and would be starting a family of his own. He is our second born; from birth, he had the biggest brown eyes and a big heart to match. He is kind and caring, and clearly a joy from the very first day.

As I took a stroll down memory lane, the photos were mainly of sports events or team photos of when he played soccer, tennis, hockey, lacrosse, and other sports. Also, there were photos of a much younger Tony who coached during healthier times. Our son was charismatic, exceptionally articulate, and confident. He often appeared sure of himself and life with him was fun and adventurous.

I thought about the first day I met his fiancée. I had just come home from work, and as I set my car keys down, I heard voices coming from the direction of the patio. When my son and his new friend came into view, I froze. As I watched, a strong sense came over me that this young lady was going to be my daughter-in-law someday and I hadn't even said "hello" yet. I went outside to introduce myself. Enjoying a steak dinner my son had prepared, they were both beaming. I could see it was a private party, so after the introductions and a few pleasantries, I excused myself.

She was precious and they appeared to be a 'match made in heaven'. Three months into their relationship she had a new tan and yet the weather was cool. I inquired, "How did you get that tan?"

She replied with a slightly raised eyebrow, "A tanning salon."

I didn't mean to bulldoze her when I said, "I would like to have grandchildren someday and you should start taking care of your womb now, so our grandchildren will not glow in the dark because of the rays of the tanning salon." Well, naturally she looked appalled, and rightfully so. I even shocked myself with that comment.

That evening, a still-very-shocked Stacey shared what I said with their friends. One of Steven's friends who had known me for years patted her on the back and simply said, "I see you have met Debbie." They chuckled at my expense. I didn't mind. My son had good friends and they all shared a great sense of humor. We all loved to laugh at ridiculous moments especially when they happened to someone else.

While still enjoying a look at the photos, his hockey picture reminded me of a very embarrassing story, again at my expense.

One day after practice, while on our way home, I noticed a shop on the main street of town and wanted to see what was inside. Steve was reluctant to go in. He said he was tired and hungry, and would just like to skip it. I thought it was a good idea because we were here right? "Let's just take a quick moment and check it out." He would rather wait in the car, but I encouraged him to come in with me and he finally conceded.

As we entered the store (it was not a shop for me at all), I wished I had never come up with the idea! The store had wall-to-wall sports paraphernalia. The tables were turned; now it was me waiting for him. As he shopped, he seemed to gain energy and forgot he was hungry. I mentioned that *I* was getting tired and hungry, and wanted to go home.

He was enjoying himself, but I grew bored very fast. On a table, I spotted a package that looked like microwave popcorn. When I picked it up, I could only see the directions which said to find the ball in the center, and with your thumb and forefinger, break the ball. I followed the instructions and broke it. The package began to swell which intrigued me. And the fact I had not paid for it yet crossed my mind.

I didn't see the other side of the package, or I would have known not to break the ball. The package continued to swell just like microwave popcorn. Suddenly my son yelled, "What did you do? Drop that and run." So, I obeyed and followed him to the exit.

When we were safe outside, I said, "Why did we run out of there?"

He said I had just activated, for lack of a better word, a *stink bomb*. He explained it would explode and that by now the whole store would stink. He continued, "Well, let's go home now. I am not going back in there to that mess."

Still completely in the dark, I said, "Mess? What mess?"

He explained that not only does it explode and stink, but it oozes brown liquid everywhere. "Yikes!!!" Once again, I was in the middle of an episode of '*I Love Lucy.*'

I didn't take time to ask him how he knew all that, but after hearing the news, of course, I wanted to bolt, too. However, I was the mom, the grown-up and to his surprise, I said, "Let's go back in. I have to make this right." As we entered the building, my son was right—the stench was unbearable; the kind that makes your eyes water and causes gagging and dry heaves. This was so embarrassing. I think I slightly threw up in my mouth. I found the sales lady by the cash register and noticed she already had a fan blowing—on full speed.

After rubbing my burning eyes, it turned out that the cashier and I knew each other. I wasn't sure if that would make the situation better or worse. She said, "Hi Debbie, I haven't seen you for a while. How are you?"

She spied Steven and without words, probably assumed he deployed the stink bomb. To get this over with, I offered an explanation, "Well, first of all, I...I...I...," while nervously stuttering, "I would like to say that it was my son who pulled this prank, but it was not. It was me."

I continued in humiliation, "I innocently activated the *stink bomb* (as I called it). I didn't see the directions. Please accept my apology." This sounded so ridiculous. I couldn't believe I was standing there pleading my case, as if that made any sense.

She listened carefully without any interruption, and I continued, "I would like to pay for it and help you clean up the mess."

To my surprise, she took full responsibility for the matter. "This was my fault for not taking them off the shelf and placing them out of reach. This has happened several times in the past, and today will be the last. I am going to move them right now!" She smiled as if she understood how difficult this was for me.

We began to laugh as we walked to the door. I thanked her for her kindness and understanding. While driving home, Steven said, "We should have bought one to take home and deploy it in the backyard for dad." I guess he wanted Tony to be part of the unique excitement, too. He said, "That *BTW*, the 'bomb', was not called a *stink bomb* that you kept calling it."

It had another more disgusting name. When he repeated the name, I said, "I wasn't wearing my reading glasses. No big deal that I didn't know the proper name of it."

Meanwhile, as I continued to view each photo, it was apparent a couple of decades had passed and it was time to face reality—the fact he was not my little boy anymore. In making peace with that, I wiped the tears from my eyes. A happy thought pulled me up from a sad place—I was not losing a son; I was gaining another daughter.

We arrived early for the wedding ceremony. Upon entering, I took in the beauty of the church and indulged in a moment to breathe in the peace I felt. One of my son's dear friends met us and ushered us outside to the back of the church to have a quiet moment with our son before his big day began. As I approached, I noticed he was sitting down, and I could see only the back of him. Memories began to flood my mind again.

I recalled the time he had to deal with his first injustice on the playground during recess. He sat by the fence and cried, "I want mommy." He was only four years old at the time and never told me about it as I am sure he thought he was alone. However, his sister had been nearby. When she told me that night, my heart sank. I could see she felt bad for him. Although, as siblings they had their share of disagreements, out in the world they stuck together.

Today he was all grown up and this was his wedding day. He turned his head and smiled at me. My heart filled with joy as I tried to fight the tears. He hugged me and comforted me as always. Then he teased that the wedding hadn't even started yet, and I was already blubbering. Through blurred vision, I began to laugh and so did he. I enjoyed one last hug from my son, the boy who turned into a man before my very eyes.

Soon the wedding began, and Tony and I were ushered down the aisle. As we took our seats in the first row, I looked up and winked and gave thanks to God. He made this day happen for our family. Tony appeared in to be good spirits and in good health for the occasion.

To add some fun to the day, the flower girls carried a sign that read, *Last chance to run, Uncle Steve.* Everyone enjoyed the humour.

The bride was radiant as she was escorted by two handsome gentlemen: her biological father, Stewart, and her stepfather, Jim. We watched our son gaze lovingly at Stacey, his wife-to-be, as she walked down the aisle. He, and everyone else, was mesmerized. She was absolutely stunning!

Both mothers were invited to do a reading. Stacey's mom, Mary, read beautifully. Then it was my turn. The reading was one of my favorites from the New Living Translation of 1 Corinthians 13:

> *If I could speak all the languages of earth and of angels, but didn't love others, I would only be a noisy gong or a clanging cymbal. If I had the gift of prophecy, and if I understood all of God's secret plans and possessed all knowledge, and if I had such faith that I could move mountains, but didn't love others, I would be nothing. If I gave everything I have to the poor and even sacrificed my body, I could boast about it; but if I didn't love others, I would have gained nothing. Love is patient and kind. Love is not jealous or boastful or proud or rude. It does not demand its own way. It is not irritable, and it keeps no record of being wronged. It does not rejoice about injustice but rejoices whenever the truth wins out. Love never gives up, never loses faith, is always hopeful, and endures through every circumstance. Prophecy and speaking in unknown languages and*

A FUN ADVENTURE

special knowledge will become useless. But love will last forever! Now our knowledge is partial and incomplete, and even the gift of prophecy reveals only part of the whole picture! But when the time of perfection comes, these partial things will become useless. When I was a child, I spoke and thought and reasoned as a child. But when I grew up, I put away childish things. Now we see things imperfectly, like puzzling reflections in a mirror, but then we will see everything with perfect clarity. All that I know now is partial and incomplete, but then I will know everything completely, just as God now knows me completely. Three things will last forever—faith, hope, and love—and the greatest of these is love.

Steven's new wife was a perfect match for him. She fits right in with all the crazy shenanigans that came with being part of our family. As I took that stroll down memory lane, I realized there were many more memories and stories that could be told, but today began a new chapter of fun and adventure for my son and his wife!

20
Love This Life

A co-worker, who is also my friend, came to work one morning with a big smile. Jill was carrying a fancy gift bag. I was wondering whose birthday it was when, to my surprise, she handed the pretty bag to me saying, "I brought this for you, Deb."

I looked in amazement at the gift now sitting on my desk and when I looked up at her, she was beaming with joy. Inside the pretty bag was a box. When I opened the lid, inside was a bracelet—a beautiful gift just for me. I put the bracelet on my wrist and thanked her for her thoughtfulness. As I looked at this unique gift, I noticed there was a charm on the bracelet. It was an anchor, the symbol of strength, from the jewelry line called *Love This Life*.

What a perfect gift, as often I prayed for extra strength. That gift became an important symbol in every situation. I wore it from then on, and during emergencies, when I felt like I was going to lose it, I would look at my anchor and it would remind me to pray for strength. I considered this lovely bracelet to be *the gift that*, as they say, *keeps on giving*. It was precious and unique, carefully chosen by a friend, just for me in my time of need, as an important reminder to *love this life!*

Although Jill was slightly mentally challenged, she was an inspiration to all who had the pleasure of meeting her, a hard worker, and genuinely caring along with all the members at our local YMCA. She was a bright light that shone in our community and her kind smile brought joy to everyone who walked through the front door!

Not too long ago this same lovely lady suggested it would be nice for us to go out for dinner someday. I took her up on her offer and we went to a nearby family restaurant. Jill had frequented that restaurant many times, and although they had great fish and chips, she suggested we try the liver and onions. She was right, the food was great and so was the conversation.

The next day, Jill mentioned to our co-workers that we had a great time and enjoyed the liver and onions. It was no surprise that our nicknames became 'liver and onions,' but we were never sure who was *'liver'* and who was *'onions.'* We simply enjoyed the humour and the joy it brought.

During a conversation with a member who was a public speaking instructor, the person asked how I was doing with overcoming my fear of public speaking. I replied, "I am ready to give up because I will never have the confidence it takes to continue, and it is time to face the fact—this is just not for me."

Jill was cleaning nearby and overheard the whole conversation. She made a comment which motivated me, "Why Debbie, you should never give up! I have a great idea. I am in the drama club, and I am in a show called the *Magical Journey* soon. Why don't you come, and I will show you how it is done!

I was honored by her invitation and agreed to go. Astonished by what just transpired, I said, "I guess, after Jill's encouraging story, I will accept her invitation and see her show, so she can show me how it is done." The instructor said even she found public speaking to be challenging. With encouragement from both ladies, I not only agreed to go to Jill's performance, but I also agreed to continue my challenge with public speaking.

"Success is not final, failure is not fatal; it is the courage to continue that counts." (Winston Churchill)

As a birthday gift for my mother, I purchased a ticket to the show for her as well. The night of the *Magical Journey* performance, Jill had dinner with us before the show. As I glanced around the room, I realized it was a sold-out event, a fundraiser, for their drama club. It was time for Jill to perform, so she left us to get into her costume. Soon she was on stage beaming with her bright smile while making eye contact with me and, in her own words, *"showing me how it is done."* She began to play *Jingle Bells* on her keyboard. A tear of joy spilled down my cheek as she showed such confidence while performing in front of an audience of about two hundred people.

It was one of the greatest shows I had ever had the privilege of seeing because of her invitation. Every one of the performers was challenged in some way and yet all appeared comfortable in front of a live audience and gave a flawless performance. When the show ended, I managed to find Jill in the crowd, and I congratulated her. I asked if she was the least bit nervous and she said, "Well, just a little, Deb" and she concluded with, "Butterflies are only normal." As a result, and over a hundred speeches later, I never cease to be grateful for Jill's encouragement.

Before the performance, I took a moment to mention to Jill's mother how Jill's encouragement made a huge difference in my life in overcoming challenges. Her mother Sue looked so proud, and she said, "Could you please call her case worker? They love to hear stories of her accomplishments." I called Jill's case worker and told her the stories of encouragement. Sometime later, Jill was honored with an award for citizen of the year!

"When we do the best that we can, we never know what miracle is wrought in our life, or in the life of another." ~ Helen Keller

Another time Jill inspired me was after an aerobics class. While cleaning yoga mats, she overheard a conversation between the fitness director and me. The director asked a question that overwhelmed me, "Would you like to take the fitness courses and become an instructor?"

At the time, we were approaching the two weddings, and going to many appointments. My mind became flooded with already too much to do as I said an outright, simple, "No."

The director was a perky redhead who spoke her mind, and as she left, she turned her head and said, "I was not expecting an answer today." That was her way of saying *'maybe no is not the right answer.'*

After the director made her exit, Jill looked up at me and, pointing to her head, said, "Debbie, it is all in your mind; you could do that you know."

I knew my answer immediately. I was going to say 'yes,' because Jill said so. I opened the studio door and I heard myself say, "I made up my mind, count me in."

She simply replied, "Okay, Deb."

After many courses and I passed the test, a dream came true: I was a certified aerobics instructor thanks to my friend Jill. About ten years earlier I wanted to become an aerobics instructor, but after a failed attempt, because I was afraid to stand in front of a group of people, I gave up. Jill helped me get over my fear of public speaking, I was now able to instruct in front of a group of people with ease.

The charm bracelet that sported the anchor, the symbol of strength, was *the gift that kept on giving* during the challenges of caregiving to come. When I felt lonely and put my head down, I would see the anchor charm as a reminder to pray and thank God for the strength He had given me, and the strength to continue to work. Most of the time, my workplace provided a pleasant social atmosphere, uplifting to anyone in the midst of adversity, with a special reminder to *love this life.*

21

DOWN THE AISLE OF MIRACLES

My daughter and I share the same favorite month: October. So, it was no surprise she picked a day in that month for her wedding. She planned to be married at Queenston Heights between Niagara Falls and Niagara-on-the-Lake with her father by her side. The ceremony was to be outside, hoping the weather would cooperate. And the reception would be inside the Queenston Heights Restaurant with a beautiful view of the Niagara escarpment and the lovely colorful trees.

Just the thought of my little girl, all grown up and starting a new chapter in her life, brought tears of joy and a tear of sadness at letting go of the fact I am no longer first in her life. I watched her grow from a quiet, gentle, caring little girl into Miss Independence, a lovely, bright, kind-hearted, and precious lady. I am proud of her and the choices she has made, yet I still have a strong desire to protect her.

I enjoyed every moment shopping with her for her wedding gown. It gave us some mother/daughter time before her big day. The gown she chose was exceptional, only adding to her natural beauty, inside and out. She was stunning. A tear managed to sneak down my cheek as I looked up at the lovely lady my daughter had become.

While she was still standing on the pedestal in her wedding gown, a bell rang to let everyone know another bride was prepared for her special day. Other shoppers and co-workers ran to see the lovely bride. It was a moment of anticipation of the day she would walk down the aisle in that beautiful gown. A moment to remember forever!

The days flew by so quickly. At last, the night of the rehearsal arrived. It was a chilly, rainy evening, but a warm, sunny day was forecast for the wedding. After the rehearsal, we shared a lovely meal at the home of her in-laws-to-be. A good night's rest was important, especially for Tony, whose health was almost in remission for the past week; God was gracious in showing His favor. As we drove home, I enjoyed the cold, rainy evening; it felt so cozy. After a good night's sleep, we arose with renewed energy in anticipation of the big day.

The sun was shining as predicted. I dashed to open the door to check the temperature; sure enough—not too hot, not too cold, just perfect. I ran back upstairs to share the news with Tony. He appeared well-rested, happy, and healthy! I read my morning devotions and thanked God for so many things, especially Tony's reprieve in health for the moment. It was a lovely drive to Queenstown Heights for our daughter's marriage on this perfect fall day.

Soon the wedding music began amidst the beauty of colorful trees, violins in harmony, and pots of fall flowers. Everyone stood as Tony proudly walked his daughter, his little princess, down the aisle. There was a special illumination over them as if God had focused the sun into a spotlight to enhance the moment. The sparkles of her dress mirrored the sparkles in their eyes. Christina appeared radiant and confident on this glorious day!

I looked up and winked and gave thanks. Tears spilled down my cheeks at the thought of the prayers answered that brought our family and friends together today.

After the ceremony, the guests were ushered to an outside patio for refreshments and the wedding party boarded a limousine for beautiful outdoor autumn photos. Tony and I left the crowd and went to the back of the building where we enjoyed a better view of the escarpment and a quiet moment together. It didn't last long. He was taking a diuretic to keep the *ascites* at bay, so we looked for the nearest open door. Although the building was not yet open for guests, we found an open door nearby, probably meant for the staff.

We entered a room on the lower level that was prepared for the ceremony in case of inclement weather. It was every bit as beautiful as the outdoor setting; they thought of everything, and I was impressed. Right outside this lovely room were two restrooms. I decided to freshen up and said I would meet him back there to continue our quiet time and admire the view before the rest of the festivities began.

All of a sudden, I heard a shuffle and then a loud thud. I looked over my shoulder and I saw shiny shoes sticking out of the men's room door. Tony had fallen and at that moment time stood still. Nothing else mattered. I ran to his shoes and the rest of him came into view, as he lay face down on the floor. He said he was fine but very annoyed. I said, "That is usually something *I* would do, not *you*. Generally, you are very sure-footed. What happened?"

His story was hilarious. He said, "I haven't seen you in a gown lately, and I was enjoying the view of your backside. Your hips in motion were so lovely I didn't see the little step. By the way, *Va Va Voom*!"

My cheeks felt hot. *Imagine, after all these years, I am standing here blushing.* I said, "Next time you are checking me out, can you be a little more careful?"

My heart was still beating loudly in my chest. I took his hand so he could feel my heartbeat. Since there was still no one in sight, we cuddled and started to laugh. We began to banter and make jokes as we always did in an uncomfortable situation. At such times we seemed to forget all about what was to come and truly enjoy ourselves. This was one of those moments to treasure.

Upon entering the ladies' room, I tried to regain my composure. I was so relieved Tony was okay and grateful for a quiet moment to refresh my makeup with still no one in sight. I was wearing my favorite color—a burgundy colored gown with nail polish and lipstick to match. I took one last look in the mirror. Although the lady looking back had weathered many storms lately, today the storms had subsided and only rainbows remained. I relished the fact that my husband still liked to *check me out* after all these years. I thanked God for this perfect day. Tony made it! It was an answer to prayer that he was able to walk our daughter down the aisle of miracles!

22

Thanksgiving

The rest of Thanksgiving weekend was rainy and perfect for curling up at home for some rest and relaxation. One of Tony's wishes was to be home for the holidays—and he was—home for Thanksgiving. There was so much for which to be grateful. We thanked God that Tony's health held up through all the wedding events in answer to our prayers.

The beautiful memories of our children's weddings felt like living through a fairy-tale with not one, but many happy endings. Our hearts were filled with joy and happiness. Today we were giving thanks. Tomorrow would be the beginning of a whole new mission.

The preliminary test results proved Tony was a good candidate for the Trillium Gift of Life list. Tomorrow the pager would arrive—another stepping stone in hopes Tony would be well again. Although we were excited, it was a little unsettling and there was the fear of the unknown.

During our last visit to Toronto General Hospital, we were told about a pager that would be sent to us. When an organ became available, we would receive a call on our home phone. If we didn't answer, the pager would beep. If we didn't respond to that, a call would be made to our children to find us. "In any event," the specialists said, "we *will* find you."

Sometimes, if the call came late at night, the recipient would be afraid, say they felt fine, and not want to have the transplant yet. *I am fine now. What if I die on the table* crossed their minds? Some just hung up out of shock and fear.

The medical team was aware of the deep emotions that caused such a reaction. A counsellor was available to help fearful patients and guide them in their decision. We were grateful to be made aware that this was normal because of fear.

After a delicious Thanksgiving dinner, we opted to retire early. In the comfort of each other's arms, I prayed for a good night's sleep as we were exhausted from all the recent events. We both had a wonderful rest. When I looked out the window the rain had stopped, and we awoke to a beautiful sunny day.

Today was the end of wonderful festivities that swept me away from the mission that was about to escalate. The pager would arrive later today making everything official. Tony looked so peaceful and comfy in our bed, so I tiptoed out of our room with my devotional books in hand.

After making a steaming cup of coffee, I wandered into the living room, lit a candle, and turned on the little electric fireplace. I opted to sit in Tony's wingback chair, wearing his comfy bathrobe with Gideon by my side. Once I was comfortable, I took a deep breath and enjoyed the afterglow of all the festivities. I wanted to make this day special for Tony rather than about the little *object* that would suddenly change our lives.

I asked God for a peaceful day to make this day special for Tony. As I read my devotions, I felt a sense of warmth and peace in that special part of the day when it was just God and me.

A little over a half hour went by when Gideon gave me a gentle nudge that he wanted breakfast. At the same time, Tony woke up. After saying 'good morning', I asked what he wanted for breakfast. He said, "Let's keep it light because we are going to return the 'father-of-the-bride' suit. I thought we could drive along the scenic route to Niagara-on-the-Lake, go out for lunch, and make a day out of it." I was impressed because usually *I* initiate any day trip. It was also a relief that he never mentioned the pager.

We quickly finished our chores ready for the drive along the Niagara River. The leaves on the trees were at their peak and the view was majestic.

Tony parked the car, and we enjoyed a stroll arm in arm. I thanked God for this perfect and *normal* moment.

At one of our favorite restaurants, we shared a meal that was *not* part of Tony's diet—a burger platter with fries and coleslaw, and a julienne salad. I had creamy Italian dressing, he opted for Thousand Island. Tony had a hearty appetite and so did I. After lunch we went for a lovely stroll and enjoyed the shops in this old fashion town.

We made our way to the bakery and ordered a date square and a medium coffee to go. Sharing a dessert and coffee was cozy and had fewer calories, too. Near the lake, we spread our blanket under a tree by the gazebo overlooking Fort Niagara. The weather was perfect and the moment quite romantic.

As we looked at the beautiful view, I could feel the peace I had prayed for. We enjoyed a quiet moment as we munched on our date square and sipped coffee. When every crumb of our treat was finished, I retrieved our books and glasses from my nice soft purse with the sparkles. After admiring it for a moment, I laid down with my feet crossed and placed my head on the purse for a pillow. It was actually comfortable. Tony sat with his legs crossed. He appeared to be happy and I was pleased.

After trying to read the same sentence three times, my mind wandered. Sometimes I could suppress the unwanted mental clutter and stay in the moment, but not today. My heart sank at the thought that when we arrived home, the pager would be waiting for us. It would be the end of the reprieve and the beginning of the new mission.

For now, I didn't want to spoil this precious moment for Tony, so I kept the thought to myself. Although we were moving forward with the hope of his good health, the thought of the pager only reminded me of the prognosis: his health will continue to decline. I looked up at him; he was watching me as if he could read my mind. His expression became more serious and finally, he said, "You know the pager should have already arrived," as he checked his watch.

I simply replied, "I know."

At that moment our love for each other grew. We held hands as if wanting to hang on to this peaceful moment. Sadly, as the saying goes, all good things must come to an end. However, I like to think that when one thing ends, a new good thing will begin. We wrapped up our picnic and all the memories, and journeyed homeward with new hopes and dreams, breathing in the beauty of the autumn leaves, without words, in utter silence.

Along the drive home, we approached Queenstown Heights where our daughter's wedding had taken place a few days earlier. Quickly I said, "Pull in. Let's go see the view of the escarpment one more time."

Beautiful flowers came into view. As we came closer, we noticed that, although the place was closed with a note on the front door 'Closed for the Season', they left all the beautiful mum flowerpots that adored the pathway where Tony had walked our precious daughter down the aisle of miracles.

Wasting no time, I asked Tony to open the trunk and back doors, because there were so many pots. He said, "Are you sure we should be taking these?"

I was a little annoyed that he acted like we were criminals stealing our own flowers. "You know we paid for these, and they were obviously left for us to take home." We gathered every pot and filled our car, front and back. I said *so long* to this wonderful place with all its fairy-tale memories. As always, Tony disapproved when I said mushy things, and then he chuckled.

Arriving back in our neighborhood, we drove to our daughter's house first and left several pots of flowers to adorn her front entrance with the memory of her wedding day. Admiring the beauty, I anticipated her surprise when she came home after a day at work. We merely turned the corner and placed several pots at another front entrance, so when the new addition to our family, our other 'daughter,' arrived home, she could enjoy the beautiful fall flowers, too.

The task completed, I gave thanks that we had shared such a nice day which set the pace for a calm moment to adjust to our new future and the pager that would become another part of our mission. When we arrived home, I opened the mailbox. Sure enough, there it was: *the pager*. The foreign object was placed on the kitchen table, and we went about our business with very few words.

23

Tender Subject

Tony and I enjoyed a whole week of bliss, but then, sadly, his symptoms came back with a vengeance. It all started one day after lunch. We had just eaten a nice meal in our bedroom. He was sitting in one of his favorite wingback chairs, evergreen with gold button strapping. With his tray on his lap, he was enjoying one of his favorite western re-runs, *Gun Smoke*. I enjoyed this show, too, as I had never seen it in the past. So, every day we would watch *Gun Smoke*, eat our lunch, have a nap, and enjoy some close time together.

All was going well when suddenly he became very confused. Within minutes things became fuzzy and unrecognizable, including his recollection of me. First, I checked his blood sugar and it was fine; he had enough fluid so I doubted it was dehydration. I called our doctor and relayed the symptoms. His directions were clear, "I will meet you both at urgent care." While driving, my concerns grew, and my stomach felt like I was being dropped from a roller coaster again.

The moment was very intense, and yet I was grateful we were meeting at our local urgent care, not too far from home. On the way to the hospital, I asked him questions starting with his own date of birth, but he didn't remember.

After a series of tests, he was transferred to Niagara Falls Hospital for further testing. When that was complete, he was admitted and we waited patiently for a room because the hospital was full at the time.

After the procedure, the nurse mentioned that it would be a while before the results came back. Tony fell asleep, so I drove home to have a rest, keep up with chores, pay the bills, and spend some time with my best friend, Gideon. Upon arrival, just the sight of my dear pet and his warm welcome made me feel better. After completing my list of responsibilities, I climbed into bed and cuddled with Gideon. I fell into a deep sleep, and when I woke up it was way past dinnertime and too late to drive out of town.

I called the hospital and Tony was still in the emergency room, sleeping. I felt guilty that I couldn't be with him. I fed Gideon and then poked through the refrigerator, opting for leftover spaghetti and meatballs. At first, I had no appetite until I smelled the aroma. I decided to take my meal upstairs and sit in Tony's chair to watch TV. If I sat in his chair, I wouldn't have to see the empty space without him, making his absence more bearable.

While carrying my dinner upstairs, I missed a step and fell. Spaghetti flew everywhere! Gideon stared at me with a goofy look, because he was waiting for me to get out of his way so he could clean up the mess. I waited a minute for it to cool. Tonight, Gideon had two dinners. I was so exhausted I climbed into bed. Even though my stomach was growling, I was too tired to do anything about it so I cried myself to sleep. I slept soundly until the alarm woke me up at 4:45 a.m. to start the day.

After letting Gideon out, I spent time in prayer and read my devotional books. Halfway through the devotional time, I let Gideon back inside to have his breakfast by my side. When it was time to leave for work, I kissed him on the snout. Often, when I was walking out the door, he pouted. I always reminded him I would be back soon. I was grateful my family lived so close because, if needed, I could always count on them to tend to Gideon. I was thankful for Gideon's companionship which helped to ward off the loneliness when Tony was in the hospital. I missed him so much it hurt, and Gideon seemed to understand my need for comfort.

After work, I came home and tended to chores. On the way to the hospital, my stomach was rumbling. Even though I had no appetite, I purchased a Junior McChicken sandwich and ice water to tide me over. As I bit into my sandwich, it tasted so good. I enjoyed it and felt no guilt that I had treated myself. When I reached the hospital, I was grateful to find a parking spot. Getting out of the car, I shook the remainder of my lunch off my clothes.

I knew I had to eat properly to take care of myself in order to take good care of Tony. My health mattered, too. His diet was a plus for both of us. Neither of us missed the salt because we became acquainted with many other ways to spice up our food. The walk from the parking lot was an opportunity for exercise, and I took the stairs instead of the elevator.

When I arrived, Tony was still in the emergency room, sleeping in a bed with surrounding curtains. A nurse said the doctor would be in shortly. When he arrived, there was no need for introductions; we had met several times when Tony's symptoms were not quite so bad. After several more tests, the doctor said it was apparent Tony was in the last stages of his illness which I already knew. I just didn't like it when people said it out loud because it would sting my heart. Toxins were entering his brain; that part was new to me. He said, "We are admitting him because there are procedures that will help."

I thanked him.

There was a lot of commotion and noise while we waited for a room and a more comfortable bed. It was a blessing when the nurse said, "Your room is ready." Minutes later, the nurse came to wheel him to his room without disturbing him. This male nurse was familiar to us and was becoming a good friend to Tony. His support for my husband pleased me. He said, "We are waiting for a private room, so in the meantime, there will be four roommates."

"We are grateful for all the help," I responded.

After settling into his new environment and sharing pleasantries with the other roommates, I left for a bit of refreshment at the Tim Horton's coffee shop, located in the lobby of the hospital. After a short break, I returned to Tony and his roommates. I noticed that two of the roommates were sleeping, another was visiting with his family, and there was Tony, looking mortified. When he made eye contact with me, he waved me over, frantically, and motioned for me to get closer because he wanted to whisper something in my ear. At first, I couldn't hear him so he became impatient and annoyed. I thought *this must be interesting*, so I listened more carefully as he whispered it again.

He said, "See that man over there in the first bed by the door."

"Yes," I said.

"Well, he told me that before they brought my bed up here, someone had died in this very spot where I am now lying and not too long ago, either."

The person who scared my husband and made him uncomfortable was now sleeping. Although another roommate was still visiting with his family, they were all staring at us as if they knew what Tony had whispered to me.

Since I had already met these folks, I felt comfortable enough to ask if they were here when someone died in this spot. With a twinge of guilt, they said, "Yes, but we were not going to tell you." They were wise, even while being swept up in this difficult conversation.

When the wife of the *informant* came back after lunch, I whispered to her not to wake up her husband and mentioned that he told my husband someone had just died in the spot where his bed was. I turned back to see a totally shocked Tony and I didn't know if it was over his situation or the fact that I just ratted this man out. She became visibly angry at her hubby. She kicked the side of the mattress with her knee to wake her husband. At first, I was sorry I mentioned it because there seemed to be a domino effect of mixed emotions.

Just when I was trying to make some sense of this unusual situation, she kicked the bed several more times. When the poor soul woke up and still appeared groggy, she swore at him and said, "Are you stupid? Why would you tell him that? We were trying not to upset these poor people."

For some reason, probably sleep deprivation, I started thinking this was like a comedy.

To lighten the situation, I said, "We were in this same room about two weeks ago and someone died in your bed." Everyone in the room got the joke and started to laugh, including the other roommate who, at some point, had wakened. There was a sense of freedom to enjoy laughter with strangers whom we would probably never see again after this incident.

During the banter and laughter, a nurse arrived with her finger to her mouth. She appeared annoyed and shushed us. She said, "This is a very tender subject and everyone in this ward can hear all of you." Then she said, quietly, "At some point, someone died in the beds you are all lying in." Suddenly everyone stopped laughing and the party was over. As she left she said, "Please keep it down," and, with a soft expression, repeated once again, "This is a tender subject."

After she left we all started to laugh even more and continued the silliness to relieve tension, only a little more quietly.

Time got away from us and I noticed it was beginning to get dark. Tony had fallen asleep, and the other visitors had gone home. I kissed Tony's forehead and walked through the long lonely, yet busy, halls of the hospital. When I left the building, it was cold outside. Sometimes it was scary to be away from home at night. I talked to God all the way to the car for comfort and as I prayed, He made things much more bearable. I appreciated our growing relationship and my fear of the dark and loneliness subsided. As I safely entered my car, I locked the door and said to God, *"Lately everything in my current life is 'a tender subject,' especially leaving my husband at the hospital and going home to our house where I miss him so painfully."*

I whispered the words out loud, "Everything is *a tender subject*," and I began to sob as I thought about all the *tender subjects* we were experiencing. Suddenly I realized that through these experiences, I was becoming a kinder, gentler, more loving soul with a tender heart. I thanked God for the pep talk and drove home thinking about all the *tender subjects*, and *these, too, will pass*. Under the illumination of the moon and the stars, I thanked God for how He was shaping and molding me for what was to come, *while we were waiting.*

24

A Christmas Story

Tony's health began to decline more rapidly. He was approaching the time the doctor warned about—*the revolving door*—a stage that would require constant visits to the hospital. As the door continued to revolve, so did my heart.

Recently, Tony's symptoms landed him in Toronto General Hospital, far from our home. One day I looked around and wondered how all these people made their way to this hospital, since none of us lived within walking distance, and most had to travel far.

When I shared my concern with the receptionist, she said, "Most people travel by way of the highway buses." That was such welcome news because it was no longer safe for me to drive the long distance while experiencing fatigue, worry, and inclement weather.

It was also mentioned that if our family physician filled out a form proving Tony's condition, I would receive the Easter Seal caregiver companion card, which would allow me to travel for free. We were so grateful for that benefit.

However, the privilege of free transportation for me, applied only when I was traveling with the patient. One morning after work, I decided to surprise Tony, so I purchased a ticket for the bus which drove me all the way to the hospital. I was grateful because it gave me ample time to rest and be refreshed for our visit.

Upon arriving, I was alarmed Tony was not in his room and nowhere to be found! I inquired at the nurses' station. Although no one knew where he was, they reassured me he was alright and probably just mobile with his walker. They added, "He is feeling a little better today and probably just wanted to stretch his legs." I was so relieved.

After all, this was a surprise visit, so Tony had no idea I was coming. I went back to his room to try to solve the mystery. When I looked out the window, I noticed a band shell. Although I could not see him, I *knew* he was there, so I quickly asked for directions because the hospital was like a small village.

I spotted him right away. Even though the nurse said he was having a good day, he looked so ill I barely recognized *my own* husband. I stepped back for a moment to suppress the tears and compose a smile. When I felt I was emotionally strong enough, I approached him. With a weak voice, he spoke first, "I knew you were coming, I could feel it. Only I was wishing you had come earlier so you could enjoy the beautiful music with me from the beginning." With a wink, He continued, "Better yet, we can make our own beautiful music together." We both began to laugh.

His laugh was so weak I could no longer keep it together. I started to cry. "I miss you so much, I can't bear it."

He said, "Me too. Not to worry. The doctor said I can go home sometime this week and I will be home for Christmas!" He took his shaky thumb and brushed away my tears.

I could no longer stop the flood. We embraced with the awkwardness of a much-distended belly separating our hug. The last of the music was beautiful and only enhanced this precious moment.

When our visit ended, I left with hope and faith that he would be home with our family for Christmas. It was cold and dark when I stepped outside the hospital. Even though the bus depot was only two short blocks away, the city seemed so scary to be walking alone at night. I moved quickly with very little energy to spare after the long day. Exhausted, I boarded the bus, grateful to be resting in a comfy reclining seat. The bus took off and I watched how busy the city was at this time of night. My broken heart sank at the thought of the distance that separated us.

I thought about Tony's wish to be home for Christmas. It gave me time to reflect that last year the same thing happened—just before Christmas we were praying Tony would be home with us for the holidays.

On the long ride home, I thought about a story I was invited to share at our church last year in front of the entire congregation about the struggles of a modern-day couple during the Christmas season.

It all began one day when I shared a personal story with our pastor. He had already been through a transplant of his own, so I felt comfortable sharing with him about a very challenging situation. When I finished, he asked if I would share this story with the congregation as part of his Christmas sermon about the struggles Mary and Joseph faced. Naturally, I said, "Please allow me to mention this to Tony before I give you an answer."

Pastor Bob said, "Of course."

Originally we declined. We were reluctant to share this particular part of our personal lives, concerned we might be judged by others. Then I realized the pastor was our friend and knew our congregation. This seemed to be so important to him. When he appeared disappointed that we turned down his request, I started to reconsider and came up with a suggestion.

"I have an idea. What would you think if I simply share the story by taking our names out of it?"

He said, "Even better, that way people can relate."

When I asked Tony for his permission a second time with the new idea, he said, "If Pastor thinks this story will be helpful to others in their struggles, then go for it!"

Since both Tony and Pastor Bob agreed, I prepared the story without our names. Sadly, when that Sunday morning arrived, Tony was still in the hospital. But there was hope because Christmas was still two weeks away. I mustered up the courage, with God's help, to share the story, while missing Tony greatly. The Christmas Speech—*Love so Amazing*

"Remember the question, 'What makes love so amazing?'

"We have a plaque in our family room that reminds us of how much God loves us. It is the Bible verse John 3:16, '*For God so loved the world that He gave His only begotten Son, that whoever believes in Him should not perish but have everlasting life'* (NKJV). What a powerful message of God's love for us and a great reminder to love others!

"Sometimes loving others isn't always that simple; in fact, it can be quite challenging at times. I would like to share a story of faith, hope, and above all, love.

"This story began at the beginning of December, while the wife was decorating the Christmas tree. In the background, a light snowfall glistened through the patio doors. She loved Christmas so much that she usually decorated a little too early each year.

"Strong in her faith, and with a soft heart, she often dreamed and wished for peace and harmony all year round. And, as we all know, life just isn't always like that. After she finished decorating, with a big smile she asked her husband, 'What do you think?'

"He replied, 'It is a dreary-looking tree. Can't you add more colour?' With that remark, she was awakened from her peaceful thoughts and immediately offended.

"She was tired of his *Eeyore* attitude. Remember the *Winnie the Pooh* character-? When any of the characters said something positive like, *'What a lovely day,' Eeyore* would reply with a negative, *'But it is going to rain.'*

"She was fed up with the *much-too-often* negative attitude. She replied with a bit of drama, 'There is nothing wrong with my decorating. You are an old grouch?'

"He replied, 'This old grouch knows enough to see that the tree needs more color.'

"They were bickering over the tree.

"Maybe you can relate: when couples are bickering over small things, there is usually a much bigger picture. She missed a significant sign—when people are depressed, even the brightest colours may look grey.

"A brief thought crossed her mind. In the past, when they had been through job loss, which usually happened right before Christmas, his spirit was low then, and understandably so. This year was different though. They were both working and there was no outstanding money issue, so why was he so glum? She thought, *well maybe he didn't love her anymore, surely that must be it.* So she said it out loud.

"'Don't you love me anymore?'"

He was dumbfounded that she would even think that. *He always loved her, even when they were disagreeing. Why doesn't she know that?*

"He snapped back, 'Of course I love you.'

"Foolishly she said, 'Well, sometimes you don't act like it.' The disagreement over *nothing* only escalated.

"Trying to fight the tears, 'I don't have to stand here and take this. I will just go to the kitchen and finish the breakfast dishes.' Before she left she noticed a cup on the end table. When she looked inside, it was half full of coffee which, by now, was cold because it had been sitting there all morning. He was still bickering. Her frustration built to a level where, normally in the past, she would stop and pray. Only this time her anger got the best of her. She picked up the cup and threw the remainder of the cold coffee in his face. (Pause) She smugly looked over her shoulder as she left the room and noticed that the coffee spilled down his face and all over the front of his sweater. He looked very angry, and she imagined at one point she could almost see steam shooting out of his ears.

"She went into the kitchen to do the dishes, and, just maybe, expected no repercussion, but she doubted it. He looked pretty upset. It was no surprise when she heard a familiar sound which she recognized immediately. It was the sound of the tree falling over; out of frustration, he either kicked it or pushed it down. Smugly, she just ignored it. She knew the sound well because she had heard it many times in the past. If the tree was off balance, it would fall. The dog knocked it over one year, and even grandma accidentally knocked it over once. Sometimes even a disgruntled person took it out on the tree—like today.

"In all the chaos she forgot he had a haircut appointment. (Pause) But *he* remembered. Before he left, he quickly changed his soiled shirt and then announced, 'I am going to get my hair cut and when I come back, the tree had better be cleaned up.'

"She replied, 'Yeah right. That is the last thing I'll do today.' Then she shouted back, 'And you better come home with a new Christmas spirit.'

"The hour he was gone did a lot for both of them; it gave them time to think. She continued her chores, except for the tree. She just stepped around it. While finishing the housework upstairs, she heard the door open and close. He was home. She also heard him pick up the tree.

"*How was she supposed to react*, she wondered. After he was finished fixing the tree, he looked for her. When he found her, he just reached for her and she reached for him, too. No words, just a necessary silence. While they were embracing, he spoke first, 'I am so sorry. I know how much you love the tree.'

"She replied, 'I love you so much and I am so sorry, too.'

"Now I love a happy ending, but we already established that life isn't always like that.

"The next day they found out why he wasn't himself lately. His health was declining and irritability was one of the symptoms. Sadly, he ended up in the hospital and his condition was not good. The first thing he said to her while lying in the hospital bed was, 'Do you think God is punishing me for knocking down the tree?'

"She reassured him. 'Of course not; it doesn't work that way. God is a God of love and mercy, not a drill sergeant ready to smack you with a big stick.'

"They began to see the humor in this situation. He conceded, 'I suppose you are right.'

"She went home and while resting, the phone rang. It was the doctor's office. She had gone through a series of heart tests and had forgotten about it with all that was happening. The receptionist said, 'We have an opening today. You need to come in.'

"Her answer was, 'I *can't* come in today. My husband is in the hospital.'

With a serious voice, the receptionist said, 'You *need* to come in today.'

"Fear took over. 'I will be in today for sure! Good-bye.' She stared at the phone a moment before hanging it up. *More drama.*

"The heart specialist's office was in the same hospital where her husband was a patient. Before her appointment, she went to spend time with him. After hugging him, she walked down what seemed to be a very long hallway. She thought, *I refuse to worry,* and again she forgot to pray. She began to panic, *Oh no, am I being punished for throwing coffee on my husband?* The tension and anxiety escalated.

"By the time she went into the office to see the doctor, she started to cry. The doctor looked puzzled. 'Why are you crying?'

"She replied, 'My husband is ill and has been admitted to this hospital, and as if that isn't enough, now you called me in to tell me something is wrong with *me*, too.'

"He looked puzzled again. 'Sometimes we call you in to tell you good news. Your tests came back fine.'

"Shocked, she said, 'Huh?' She thanked him and couldn't run quickly enough to tell her husband she was alright.

"When she got to her husband to tell him her news, she was surprised to see the doctor was there and her heart sank. Suddenly she remembered to pray, and also remembered that sometimes the doctor brings good news. Surprisingly, the doctor said, 'I have good news. Your husband is doing miraculously well and he can go home tomorrow.'

"She thanked the doctor and smiled at her husband. It melted his heart. Then she looked up and gave praise and thanks to God for His blessings.

"Two weeks later it was Christmas. The couple sat at the table surrounded by their family. For a moment they looked across the table with a sparkle in their eyes and smiled at each other, remembering how blessed they were. They were so much in love.

"The original question was: What makes love so amazing?

"It is a gift from God, a precious gift that doesn't come wrapped in a pretty package with a big bow. It is a free gift to anyone who wants to receive it.

"It is *the gift that really does keep on giving* because that couple had many more challenges to face in the future. With the special gift of God's love, their love for each other grew to a new level.

"I would like to close with these words:

'*And now these three remain: faith, hope and love. But the greatest of these is love*' (1 Corinthians 13:13, NIV).

"Romans 8:28 (NIV) says, '*And we know that in all things God works for the good of those who love him, who have been called according to his purpose.*"

After the Christmas speech, not one church member inquired if the story was about us. Although we *were* the characters in the story, it was much better for people to relate to the story without our names being mentioned.

That Christmas Tony did make it home for Christmas, and, once again, we shared a holiday we both knew was a precious gift from God. As we were swept up in the midst of our chaotic Christmas dinner, passing dishes of delicious food, surrounded by our family, there was an unsaid understanding when we took a brief moment to stare into each other's eyes and give God thanks. There it was: our Christmas miracle—Tony was home for Christmas!

25

WATCH YOUR STEP

On my fridge is an erasable note board. Before I purchased this, I would run the growing list of chores through my mind, hoping not to forget anything. I hoped this board would take the pressure off my mind, disciplining myself to write down all the chores and responsibilities in order of importance.

I would start at the top and complete the most important task first. Then there was no room for procrastinating. The results were amazing. Naturally, Tony's care came first; there was a sense of relief as each task was done. The *priority list* provided the balance necessary for my workload.

It was the first week of January and my task today was to put away the Christmas decorations. After reading my devotional books, and savoring a hot cup of coffee, it was time to get to work. I knew Tony would be sleeping for at least another hour, so there was ample time to get a head start on the day.

I gathered all the decorations, very careful not to break any, as some were over fifty years old. I was actually enjoying the process and the precious memories that came with each piece. For a moment, there was a sense of normalcy.

Suddenly reality returned when Tony abruptly called my name with urgency in his voice. Stepping around the boxes blocking my path, I ran up the stairs and groaned after banging my hip into the banister, knowing there would be a bruise, but kept going. Even when I had proper rest, sometimes there was still fatigue from the emotional stress, and in the rush, I often got hurt.

When I saw him, I knew he was in discomfort, because he was covered in a mucky puddle. After examining him, it appeared there was leakage spilling through the dressing. I called the hospital where we had already spent a portion of last night while they did a procedure to relieve the pressure of the water in Tony's belly. Once again, we would be on our way to *the revolving door* of the hospital.

I helped him dress and managed to get him into the car and off to the hospital in record time. It was important the small incision from the procedure be treated and not become infected. Niagara Falls hospital was now our *second home*. When Tony was comfortably seated in a wheelchair, I went to park the car and noticed that for January, the weather was clear and calm.

They stitched up the problem and we headed for home. The calm weather changed; the sky became dark and grey to mimic our dispositions. By the time we were in our driveway, it started to rain. I got Tony safely into the house and settled in his comfy chair. Refreshing the bed was *not* on my perfect list.

The disarray of Christmas paraphernalia still awaited my attention. I made lunch and then helped a very fatigued Tony into bed. He enjoyed his lunch on a bed tray and watched *Gun Smoke*. I sat in his wingback chair. Actually, I *collapsed* in his chair.

When I glanced at Tony, he just stared at his plate. I knew by his face he had no appetite. So, mindlessly, I sat on the side of the bed and spoon-fed him. After finishing most of his meal, he fell asleep and so did I. Rest was very important to us both to keep up our strength. So, usually after lunch, I would curl up next to him and nap, too.

An hour later, I cleaned up the lunch dishes while Tony continued to nap. Since his favorite down blanket was soiled, another chore was added to the growing list. I decided to go to the corner Laundromat to use the heavy-duty machines for oversized items. Before I left, I checked on Tony one more time.

I gathered the blanket and detergent, and *why not grab some recyclables, too?* My arms were so full I knew I should make two trips. But, oh well. I walked outside and didn't realize the entire town had frozen over when I made a plunge down the front steps.

In the process, the heel broke off my shoe. I lay on our front lawn in excruciating pain with freezing rain pelting down on my face. For the first time, I wished one of my neighbors was watching my *stooge act* because this time I needed help—but there was no one around. My little neighborhood was desolate.

I closed my eyes, stinging from the elements, and said, "*God, I am too exhausted for words so, quite simply, it is just You and me. I am counting on You to literally carry me through this situation.*" I started to crawl up the stairs when suddenly the door swung open and Tony was standing in the doorway. Apparently, my *not-so-ladylike* fall made such a thud it woke him and he was looking down at me, asking if he could help.

I was frustrated, because of my concern for him. Now we were both hurting. I said I was fine even though the condition of my ankle and other bruises had not yet been diagnosed. To keep him from stressing about me, I sugar-coated the situation and crawled up the icy stairs like a tarantula. I was in so much pain. My clothes were damp and cold, but I inched to the middle of the living room to assess my injuries.

Very concerned, Tony offered to drive me to the hospital, but he had not driven for some time. So I mustered up a casual, "I am fine," hoping my answer would ease his mind. "I just need to borrow your cane. See, my right foot is still okay." I ended up barefoot, so needed proper footwear to go back out into the ice storm to get medical attention. My left foot was so swollen I could only fit into Tony's sneaker; so, we made do. I wore a boot with traction on the other foot.

Off to the hospital I went for the third time in 24 hours. While I waited, I noticed many other folks had fallen in the storm as well. There was a broken shoulder and a broken tailbone, just to name a few. I was grateful the x-ray revealed the ankle was badly sprained but not broken. The doctor on call was aware of our situation, as Tony was a *frequent flyer* at this hospital. So it was thought best to try Extra Strength Tylenol for the pain in order to keep alert to take care of Tony, and now myself.

I made a brief stop at the grocery store, hobbling around with Tony's sneaker on one foot and my boot on the other. When I arrived home, I was confronted by the mess of what started the whole thing. It began on our front porch, came down the stairs, and ended on our front lawn. Normally I would stop to make everything look perfect again, but the idea was abandoned by the severe pain in my ankle. So, I limped over the mess and hobbled into the house.

Another mess came into view. Again, I discarded perfection and stepped unsteadily over the original disarray of Christmas decorations that didn't miraculously put themselves away. It was now dinnertime, so I prepared our meal and rested with Tony, pleased to see he had an appetite. After dinner, I took my second dose of Extra Strength Tylenol and went to work. I was able to work while sitting on my living room floor and tried to recreate what our home once looked like on a good day while resting a very tender ankle.

Suddenly I was startled by the sound of the doorbell. It had slipped my mind Tony's nurse had called to let us know he would be arriving within the hour for their routine visit. I pulled myself up somehow, groaning in pain, and, with no energy, answered the door.

Usually quick-witted, he said, "Hey, Deb, were you guys evicted?" Obviously, he saw the mess outside. Normally I would appreciate his humor, but before I could speak, he looked around and made another joke. "Are you on some sort of a roll?"

Finally, I spoke, "Ha, ha, very funny. Normally I appreciate your humor, but today I have to admit is not a good day. In fact, it is a very bad day."

Quickly I explained. After all, he was here to see Tony, not me. It sounded like another *I Love Lucy* episode. He looked very concerned and said, "Let me look at that ankle."

I said, "No worries, it is okay." He reminded me a sprain can be more painful than a break.

"Try to find some time to stay off it," he suggested.

While he attended to Tony, I sat on the floor, trying to clean up a mess which seemed like I had begun to do a week ago. As I wrapped the Christmas decorations in a newspaper, I started to feel sorry for myself. Only through God's strength did I escape teetering over the pit of despair.

The thought crossed my mind that I could have called for backup from family, neighbors, or friends who would have been happy to help. Then I realized I had all the signs of distancing myself from everyone. With no energy left, I was not sure how to correct the *'I've got this'* syndrome, so I sat and cried.

There was so much stress. The discomfort of our situation was compounded by comments people made that would shock me. While shopping, I was often stopped by concerned people who would *interview* me. They would ask, "What are you going to do if he doesn't get a transplant?" My heart would sink, and I wondered, *is that inane question supposed to be helpful?*

After these unscheduled events, not only was I bruised physically, but emotionally as well. Being distant from people made the load even heavier. With a tear-stained face, I decided that from this point on, I would try to include others in our moments of need and be mindful at all times to *watch my step*!

A few weeks later, Tony was hospitalized again with new symptoms. I left the room to hide the flood of tears at the thought of the tremendous weight this mission had become. A caring person stopped to ask why I was crying. I hemmed and hawed and I finally said, "My husband is in that room and soon he will be coming home in my care again. Since he has no muscle tone left, he is wobbly, and there are often toxins in his brain so he can no longer think clearly. I am afraid if he falls, he will miss his chance for the transplant." I cried even more at the thought.

Gently, she put her arm around my shoulder and introduced herself as the director of home care. "When your doctor signs the papers, a whole new world, and many doors will open for you!" I trusted this complete stranger and thanked her.

Instantly relief washed over me, and my stress level decreased at the thought of assistance with home care for Tony. I was so grateful that my tears changed to tears of joy! As we parted, she noticed my limp and when she inquired about it, I said, "I'm fine, just fine!"

My concern was alleviated when our family doctor signed the papers. The next day someone from home care arrived at our door to explain the benefits they would be providing.

Soon after all kinds of equipment: railings to be installed, and a fancy chair that lifted Tony up electronically. Our bedroom was soon transformed into a hospital room. I was so thankful for the safety measures being provided. Now we would both need to *watch our step*!

26

DISCOURAGEMENT AND DESPAIR

As his wife, I knew how I felt, but could not fully understand what was going through Tony's mind as we journeyed toward this mission. So I asked about his thoughts and feelings. Here is what he was going through.

I could feel myself slowly dying from the disease. Even though my wife said the whole town was praying for me, I thought all the prayers in the world would not help me if God wanted to take me. Discouragement, hopelessness, and despair set in with a vengeance. While lying there countless times in the same hospital, I realized all the encouraging words could not change the final outcome if there is no organ for me. I felt like I was in the dark, and had been forgotten, after waiting more than a year *on the list*.

I could not control my disappointment any longer. While my family was visiting, I could not even pretend to have a good attitude. One day my sister, Anna, and her husband, Don, tried to console me. I knew this was unbearable for them to witness. After they left, the nurse came in with medication and I refused to take it because—what was the point? I hit rock bottom, and as hard as I tried, I could not climb out of the *'pit'* into which I had fallen.

Just then my wife came in and I told her how I felt. She tried to lift my spirits but, by this time, they were just too shattered. I didn't realize she had another plan. She understood and knew we were dealing with a broken spirit and discouragement. She said, "We need back up." At that moment she glanced toward the hallway and spotted someone. As she ran out the door, I heard her say, "We have an emergency here, we have a broken spirit," and she came in with a visitor whom she already knew to be the chaplain at the hospital. It was at that God-given moment he happened to be walking down the hallway.

He introduced himself as Reverend Bond also known as *'Double O Heaven'*. Apparently, that was his icebreaker which he borrowed from the movie *James Bond 007*. My wife got a kick out of this immediately, but I was so miserable I didn't think it was funny at all. After he left, my wife said, "You looked at him like a bug to be squashed. Did he say anything that was helpful?"

"No, I feel worse!"

My wife looked disappointed because she hoped that kind man would be able to help me.

As the day went on, I recalled that when I told him I had given up, he told me he had seen many people in my position who had pulled through quite well and were living normal lives. So just try to keep that in mind and hold on to it.

Deb stayed long and endless hours by my side, often quiet. Although she appeared upbeat, I knew it was just for my sake. I could see the stress on her face, and she looked exhausted. It was getting late and dark outside. I worried about her and what would happen to her if I didn't make it. She often waited for me to fall asleep and then left, as she had to get up early for work the next day. Only tonight I was not sleepy, I was agitated. She held my hand and prayed for us both.

The following day was my birthday. A whole year had gone by since the specialist said, "I never gave you my gift, so today I am going to give you your birthday present. We are going to put you on the Trillium Gift of Life List."

Those words lingered in my mind as my optimistic wife said, "Maybe today will be our special day," but she still had a strained look on her face that was apparent almost all the time now.

Then our immediate family stampeded through the door to celebrate what may be my last birthday. Debbie's expression softened. She was thrilled to see everyone with balloons and cake. It was a relief to see her genuinely happy. And I got another gift—we were going to be grandparents.

It was quite apparent our daughter and daughter-in-law were getting closer to their due dates. Where did the time go? With the balloons, cake, family, and the smile on my wife's face, I began to feel hopeful again. Today the gift I received was that there is much to be thankful for. With Deb's hand in mine, we would continue this mission with hope for a wonderful future together!

27

A WEEK OF BLISS

The disease had taken its toll on Tony's other organs which were beginning to shut down; his kidneys were now in distress and his liver was in complete trauma. Sadly, we understood the warning signs. Tony was to be placed in palliative care without any hope of his returning home unless he received his *Gift of Life*. The hospital chosen was close to home so the immediate family could be by his side day and night. In the midst of grief and sorrow, my strength was my trust in God.

The next day was Sunday. While I was at church, right in the middle of the sermon, I had an overwhelming feeling something was not right. Quickly I gathered my belongings and went straight to the hospital. Upon entering my husband's room, it was clear he had become completely unresponsive. The nurse came into the room seconds later and said they were just getting ready to call me; she confirmed the doctor was on his way.

Minutes later the doctor arrived and immediately examined my husband, who just lay there lifeless and motionless. As the doctor shook his head from side to side, appearing very serious, I read his body language all wrong, thinking I had lost my husband.

I was in complete disbelief, when the doctor said, "He is okay, just not responsive." I wiped the unstoppable stream of tears and thanked God Tony was still with us. We were already warned that while waiting for an organ transplant the patient may go into a coma or become unresponsive. My level of hope and trust only increased, believing he would soon receive a miracle. I was comforted by the thought it was just a matter of time.

As Tony's condition declined, our family doctor and the specialist worked together to give him the gentle care he needed. With orders from the specialist in Toronto, Tony was transferred to Niagara Falls Hospital for further care and testing. While the doctor and nurses worked diligently to revive him, I was never asked to leave the room. I remained by his bedside in utter distress, praying for him to wake up.

Around 11:00 in the evening he finally awoke from the fog he was in. He smiled at me and for that moment I knew he was temporarily *out of the woods*. When he was resting comfortably, I left to go home. The cool night air revived me. I unlocked my car door, and climbing in, I thanked God that Tony's condition was stable once again.

After the half-hour drive home, I crawled into bed, set the alarm, and fell into a deep sleep only to be awakened by the screech of the alarm at 4:45 a.m. Bewildered, I scrambled out of bed and got ready for the early morning shift. I was only working three shifts a week and for only three hours. I had downsized to part-time when the time was right to help Tony.

While I was working, I had peace of mind because home care provided everything we needed and more. Not only did they provide equipment, proper furniture, hand railings, and bed rails, they assigned nurses who didn't mind the early shift to watch over Tony while I was at work. We were blessed to have such great care for him.

Home care was a huge blessing in countless ways, and I was able to keep my job where I was still fairly new. During the course of the day, there was a parade of nurses, and our family doctor who made house calls, to keep Tony stable until his surgery. However, when he went into the hospital, all services came to a halt.

A few lonely days went by. When I wasn't at the hospital or at work, I would spend the time in our bedroom resting. Often people would say, "Well, it must be nice to have a break." I didn't feel like it was *a break* because I missed him so much. In his absence, everything seemed to shut down, including me, until I saw him again. I would lie in our bed completely exhausted, isolating myself from everybody and everything. I became a recluse.

It was early in the morning when the phone rang. To my amazement a nurse was calling to say, "Your husband has miraculously taken a turn, and for the better! There is no reason he should stay in the hospital any longer. You can come to pick him up today." I was elated and thanked her, saying, "I will be right there." To our delight, Tony bounced back and was able to return home! It was a miracle—to have the gift of more time to share with my husband.

I felt a sense of joy and was eager to bring him home. A call to home care to let them know we would need the benefit of their services again. The house was tidy and cheerful for his arrival. I spruced myself up and applied fresh makeup to hide the evidence of my emotions.

On the journey back to the hospital, I thanked God for this unprecedented event to share more precious time with my husband. The nurse wheeled him to the car and home we went—right to his comfy bed, secure again within our own four walls.

After he was comfortable, I climbed into bed, too, just to be by his side. My arms ached to cuddle him only he was so fragile. It was just too uncomfortable for him to be embraced or even held at this point, so I just kissed and cuddled his face, ever so grateful he was home. I massaged his feet with moisturizer for touch therapy which he enjoyed.

As I continued to rub his feet, he fell into a deep sleep, and I thanked God for many things. Lying next to my husband, I noticed his heartrending features and prayed for God's comfort for him. Suddenly, sleep overcame me, too, and I fell into a nice rest. It was understood that I was on call for 24-hour duty and could easily be awakened at the slightest sign of any distress.

The very next day he woke up refreshed and said, "I feel pretty good." I was elated for him yet confused at this turn of events. He continued, "I would like to go on one of those day trips that we so enjoy."

Naturally, I was happy about this change and yet very perplexed. I said, "Sounds great, let me check with the doctor first." He smiled.

I called the specialist's office in Toronto. "Tony wants to go on day trips and enjoy going out for a meal. Is that possible?"

The receptionist placed me on hold and when she returned, said, "The doctor said at this point he can do whatever he would like to do!" I thanked her, hung up the phone, and ran to Tony with the good news.

We were both excited about this blessing—a reprieve! "Where would you like to go?"

He said, "What are my options?"

Gladly, I named four choices: Niagara-on-the-Lake including lunch and a date square from the old-fashioned bakery; Niagara Falls to the indoor botanical gardens including a homemade picnic lunch at Dufferin Islands; Niagara Falls to the Wild Bird Kingdom; or Port Colborne for fish and chips and a view of the canal. All four had some things in common—delicious food, a sense of being on vacation, and the benefit of being only a short drive away.

During this week of bliss, with the help of a walker and a wheelchair, we managed to enjoy all four choices. It was amazing. We savoured every minute of our time together, encouraging each other that our miracle *would* happen. We enjoyed the best time ever!

The morning after the festivities were over, I was awakened from our bliss to the cold reality this reprieve was only temporary. It was no surprise that my stomach had the sensation of plunging down the giant hill on a roller coaster again. All my emotions were plunging down, too, as I was starting to fall into the pit of despair.

Suddenly, I decided to call the Trillium Gift of Life Network in hopes of relieving some of my concerns. Just to hear a voice from Toronto, the place that offered *the Gift of Life*, gave me some perspective and support in hopes of relieving the sensation we were just floating in the abyss.

The lovely lady at the other end of the call was so caring. After I explained our situation, she understood, and instantly I felt relief. I told her we realized it was a privilege for Tony to be on the list; yet, at the same time, discouragement just set in because his MELD score dropped to a number that was no longer in the red zone and I thought it meant he would have to wait even longer.

She listened carefully; she was my lifeline of support, and the reason I was able to hold it together. She understood the term MELD—the acronym for *Model for End-stage Liver Disease*. A MELD score is a number from six to forty, based on lab tests.

I shared our story of the blissful week and how we were having fun in the midst of this extraordinary time and enjoying humor that was such good medicine for our aching hearts. Because his MELD score had dropped, I was suddenly brought back to reality. I felt crushed and defeated but not forgotten, just lost. I started to sob.

Confidently she said, "Why, my dear, this is the week that we wait for. He was much too ill to survive surgery when his MELD score was in the red; now he is strong, and that is usually when the patient will receive his call." Then she said to be prepared for that day and what to expect.

She continued, "First, the call usually occurs in the middle of the night. Upon receiving the call, many people like you and your husband are experiencing a moment of reprieve. They explain how well they feel and ask us to call another time, and then hang up before we can respond. Although this is what they were waiting for, there is the fear they could die while in surgery, so it is only natural to want to cling to the precious time they have. We understand this common reaction."

I felt comforted when she said, "At this stage of the illness, we begin to receive many calls from concerned family members." I thanked her for her time and reassurance. Her last words were, "You never know, tonight could be the night."

"Interesting, because I was at the local hair salon today and when the staff and customers inquired about Tony's condition, I said, 'You never know, tonight could be the night,'" We were both amazed. It was a perfect moment with a kind, caring person and I no longer felt like I was floating in the abyss.

I hung up the phone with a new sense of optimism and the ability to continue our week of bliss. Tony and I shared a perfect day of peace, joy, and surprisingly, laughter. His laughter took such a weight off my heart as we continued to banter. Once again, I could feel the power of the prayers many people in our town were saying on our behalf.

During dinner, we enjoyed eating our meal on TV trays as we watched a movie. I chose an old movie that usually gave us belly laughs. It was titled *"What about Bob"* a zany comedy with co-stars Bill Murray and Richard Dreyfuss. I noticed an absence of stress in Tony's expression. It was good to see he had an appetite today and enjoyed every morsel of his dinner, and so did I. We laughed while watching the movie and my heart felt lighter at this very special moment. I looked up and winked.

After dinner, with full bellies, both from food and laughter, we retired for a good night's rest. Before turning out the light, we prayed together and gave thanks for this week of bliss. We drifted off for a pleasant peaceful rest. It was a welcomed surprise when the phone startled us around midnight. We both sat up and announced to each other in unison, *"This is it!"*

28
TRILLIUM GIFT OF LIFE NETWORK

Although the phone was next to Tony, he didn't pick it up—maybe in shock. So, I crawled around him, picked up the receiver, and said, "Hello." A kind, gentle voice confirmed that this indeed was *the call* we had waited for so long—*The Trillium Gift of Life Network*. I felt it was important for Tony to hear the news firsthand, so I gently placed the phone in his hand so he could hear the peaceful way this moment was presented to him.

The person spoke calmly with a hint of cheerfulness as they prepared us to get to Tony's destination.

After we hung up the phone, there was no time to waste pondering, since part of our instructions was to be at the hospital by 4:30 a.m. and it was already a little past midnight. I called both our daughter and son, but there was no answer. So, I called an ambulance.

By the time we were ready to leave, the ambulance, fire truck, and police had all arrived and lit up the front of our house.

In the midst of all the pandemonium, our son suddenly appeared. He was able to drive between the commotion and come right up to me. With strength and confidence, he said, "We are ready to go."

Steven and Stacey were our escorts; I was relieved and so pleased. I said, "I will go to get your dad," grateful at how quickly this whole event was unfolding.

Soon I ushered Tony and his belongings into the car while thanking *the cavalry* that was still lighting up our house and woke our neighbors. To those looking on, I gave the thumbs up as we drove off. Eventually, Steven asked, "Why were all those emergency vehicles at your house?"

I said, "They have been a major part of our lifeline and I guess if you call one, they all show up."

Our family drove off into the night and everyone in the car remained calm, at peace, and very supportive. Due to the hour, there was little traffic on the highway, so we arrived at the hospital in good time. As we entered the front door, I could feel a strong sense of peace and calm come over me. I knew that *everything was going to be alright*. Tony appeared strong and ready emotionally.

After admission, registration, and paperwork, we were sent to a room with a leather fold-out sofa and two leather chairs that reclined. Several nurses went to work taking blood samples. One of them asked, "Is this your first call for the transplant?"

Tony said, "Yes."

As I wondered what difference that made, it was clarified. "Well, sometimes after testing we discover that this match is not right for you, and we call the next in line. They may call you back several times before this will actually happen for you." In other words, this may not happen today.

We understood but were still very hopeful. Soon after all the tests came back the announcement was made, "This is a perfect organ for you, but the surgery has been postponed from 4:30 to 6:30 this morning."

So, we all took our places. Steven and Stacey reclined in the chairs; Tony and I were on the fold-out bed. Before we all napped, I kept our daughter, Christina, and her husband Jay, informed by phone about the change of events, as they were waiting for their instructions as well. We also kept in touch with Tony's siblings and my mom and sister. Our pastor was informed and our situation was sent to the prayer chain of our church immediately.

At some point, we were informed that the surgery was postponed until 12:30 p.m. which gave Steven and Stacey time to have breakfast.

When they returned, we had more news. The surgery was now scheduled for 3:30 this afternoon, with the possibility it may be postponed again.

We were told there was a hotel close by that offered immediate family members of chronically ill patients a fifty percent discount. This was not an option for me, because at this point the doctor said, "We work hour to hour." In other words, anything could happen at any time. So I stayed close by Tony's side. We just lay on the fold-out sofa while Steven and Stacey rested in the two recliners.

Eventually, the surgeon came to let us know the surgery would take place at 6:30 that evening. As he explained the delay, we dismissed our thoughts about the reason we were there in the first place. All our focus went to the family whose loved one was on life support with no hope of recovery. Then the surgeon said, "There is still hope for this surgery to happen for you; it is just a matter of time."

Suddenly what we had waited so long for was gladly put on hold as we shared a moment of grief and sympathy for the other family involved.

The Trillium Gift of Life List often meant someone else died, and their organs were being shared to give life to another person—a gift of life soon to be shared with Tony.

We began to suffer emotionally for the family of the person who had died in a car accident. The person was transported to the Trillium Gift of Life Centre on life support to keep the organ fresh until the recipient arrived for the transplant. The accident victim and the patient were en route at the exact same time.

The tender part was when the doctor continued with this very painful explanation of the delay. "The family of the deceased is confused by the life support as they believe there is still hope that their loved one will wake up. Because it happened so fast, the family needs time to make peace with the fact that their loved one is gone." With that, I could no longer hold it together and I started to sob.

Although we knew that the donor would have to die, it hit home like a whirlwind. This is real and when I glanced at Tony to see how he was doing, he, too, looked forlorn and bewildered at the thought of the grief and pain the other family was experiencing. There is a term used for this moment called 'survivor's guilt', a condition of emotional pain for the ones who survived and for the transplant recipient.

What were we thinking? *Did we think these organs grew on trees and we just picked the right one?* The doctor continued, "There is a grief counsellor with the family right now, and since it is up to the family to make the decision when to remove the life support, this surgery time may be postponed again. The doctor left the room and we both felt extreme loss for the other family.

It was no surprise when we were told the surgery was postponed until the next morning. With that news, it was time to send Steven and Stacey home as we did not want our pregnant daughter-in-law sleeping in a recliner one more night. Although they did not want to leave us, Tony and I insisted. As I watched them go, I started to cry from the strain of all that was involved—the extreme pressure and the fact I missed them immediately even though it was right to send them home.

At the Trillium Gift of Life Network, donor and recipient matching is conducted 24 hours a day, 365 days a year. Once a donor is deemed suitable, TGLN's computer system matches the donor's organs to that of the patient on the waiting list. When matching organs there are a number of factors to consider including blood type match, medical urgency, and the size of the organ(s) needed. The matching criteria are developed by members of the transplant community and approved by a provincial Transplant Steering Committee.

Also, TGLN is committed to creating a system that enables every person in Ontario to make an informed decision about organ and tissue donation and to support healthcare professionals in implementing those decisions.

After the news of the delay, our hearts were completely shattered by the pain of what the other family was experiencing. We were emotionally exhausted. So Tony and I rested in complete silence, praying for God's comfort for the grieving family. It was no longer about us or our survival; it was about the compassion and care for everyone involved in this incredibly extraordinary moment in time.

Shower Us with Flowers

Some time ago instead of stepping into the pit of despair, I spent time in prayer at a chapel in Niagara Falls. That night in the middle of a deep sleep, I was awakened by the powerful scent of flowers. Grateful for this fragrant gift, I delighted in the comfort it brought as I continued to breathe in the wonder of this delicate moment.

Naturally, I looked around the room to see if there was an earthly source and to my surprise there was none. The welcome fragrance was similar to the scent of roses with an uncanny musty smell, almost ancient. I could not compare the scent to anything else and continued to breathe in the gift while it lasted.

The doctor arrived and said, "Your surgery has now been scheduled for 6:30 tomorrow morning, with no more delays. And we will move you to a private room." After more instructions, he left. I packed up Tony's bag full of everything I could think of that he might possibly need.

My possessions were very few because I left the house almost two days ago with my purse and just the clothes I was wearing. When we arrived at the hospital, there was uncertainty about the time of the surgery, so I mentioned this to a nurse and was offered a 'bath in a bag' and other necessities. She said, "We also take care of the family." That kindness melted my heart and a tear of gratitude slid down my cheek.

Months earlier, as the family of a patient, we were offered a hotel room, within walking distance of the hospital, at a fifty percent discount. Since we were working hour to hour, this offer was not the answer for me. I needed to stay close to Tony to wait for instructions.

The evening hours came upon us swiftly. In the privacy of our room, our conversation was light; we spent our last few moments simply encouraging each other. In the midst of grim reality, there was the hope of new life. We understood that after the surgery some patients never respond and some pass away shortly after. This was a very real and delicate subject.

We were both fatigued and went into our usual coping mechanism—banter. Although I was given a reclining chair for rest and sleep, I climbed into bed with my husband to comfort us both. When we drew close, he said, "Do you think they will delay the morning surgery?"

I replied, "I think this will happen and you will become healthy again." I had a strong feeling that, to quote Tony, *everything was going to be alright.*

After what felt like a long nap, there was that familiar scent of musty roses as strong as ever, the exact same scent I remembered from long ago, and with it came the feeling of comfort and peace. But now it was a shared experience. Suddenly a nurse arrived with a gurney to take Tony for surgery. I noticed him pause to take a breath and I asked if he noticed the strong scent. He continued to sniff the air. "Yes, it smells like a bouquet." He, too, could sense the comforting fragrance.

I said, "I believe it is a scent from heaven and God's way of letting us know *everything is going to be alright.*"

The nurse replied, "Rarely have I smelled that scent in the thirty years I have worked here. Never have I heard it put into words. I believe you may be right, a scent from heaven." He was taken by the fragrance, too.

Tony was quietly enjoying the scent and this extraordinary moment as well. Between the fragrance and the kind nurse, a bubble of peace formed around us. I said, "I can feel the power of all the people praying for us right now and we are so grateful."

The time had come to leave the room where we spent our last moments together. As we walked down the hallway, I held Tony's hand as the scent of the bouquet dissipated. We journeyed through many doors and finally, one elevator took us to *the double doors*—the moment for which we had waited so long. In our last few seconds together, we silently thanked God for the peace and comfort of this moment and for showering us with flowers.

30

GATEWAY TO A NEW BEGINNING

Anticipation grew at the sight of the doors to the operating room which offered Tony hope for a healthy future. It was the *gateway to a new beginning* for us.

The attendant gave us ample time to encourage each other in the last few precious seconds. We had been 'joined at the hip,' side by side, for so long, it was only natural the thought of parting pained my heart. With God's help, I remained as strong as possible for Tony. Since he appeared brave, confident, and ready, I wanted to mirror his positive attitude as his support system, but it was not easy.

He reached for a kiss, and then we kissed several more times. To lighten the moment, the attendant said, "I could leave you two alone, but there is a team of about thirty people who are waiting for you."

Tony kissed me again and in between kisses he said to the attendant, "Maybe you better leave." We both laughed a little nervously and then I watched him be taken away, never taking our eyes off of each other till he was out of sight.

He was now in a place where I could no longer be by his side, no longer hold his hand, nor have a lingering kiss. The pain I tried so desperately to contain in order to be strong for Tony, instantly dissolved into a 'tsunami' of tears spilling into an ocean of overwhelming and long-time coming deluge of emotion. I was crushed, completely alone, and whaled out loud in my grief.

Tony's experience:

After telling Debbie that I love her one more time, we entered *through the double doors.* I noticed so many people in the operating room waiting for me to arrive. I looked around and thought *all these people are going to be working on me!* Everyone was so relaxed and pleasant like they had done this procedure a hundred times, which they probably had.

The anesthesiologist introduced himself. All the nurses and the surgeon approached me with positive comments trying to reassure me that *everything would be alright.* After some preparations, one of them asked me if I was scared. Quite frankly I wasn't scared; I was more nervous than anything else. This was the beginning of what we were waiting for.

As I lay there waiting for the anesthetic to take effect, I felt calm and relaxed. I happened to look to my left, just a couple of feet away and saw one of the doctors cleaning something in a silver pan that appeared to be my new liver. I couldn't see all of it, but just enough to see him cutting away some of the fatty tissue.

I asked him, "How does it look?"

He turned to me and said with such confidence, "It looks great. This is a very healthy and a very good liver." I felt so relieved and grateful. He told me that when the operation was over, he would see me in the recovery room so he could answer any questions I may have.

He reassured me everything would work out. As I took one final look around, they lowered the huge overhead lights closer to me and said, "Count backward from one hundred."

"Ninety-nine, ninety-eight, ninety-seven, ninety-six, ninety…"

While still standing by *the double doors* another attendant was on his way to usher me to the surgical waiting room. He suddenly appeared. After many years of experience escorting family members, he was well prepared for this moment. As we walked together, I talked about faith and hope and he began to quote powerful, familiar, scripture verses; he, too, had a strong faith in God.

Approaching the surgical waiting room, I saw large windows overlooking the lobby, normally a very busy area, but today it was so early in the morning that there were very few people, just a few employees busily cleaning the area before the crowd would eventually arrive.

As we looked through the window, night began to turn into day. Suddenly the room was filled with sunlight and a feeling of peace came over us. Once again there was that powerful sensation that *everything was going to be alright*. I sniffled a little more, dried the remainder of my tears, and thanked the kind gentleman who was obviously just the right person for this job.

I noticed that both attendants were heavily decorated with pins. I learned they were symbols of acknowledgement for their front-line duty of keeping the patient and families grounded as they became separated by *the double doors*. I was so grateful for the comfort and support of the two men whom both had a strong faith in God.

After a few more pleasantries to make sure I was alright, the attendant left to go back to other patients and surgeries scheduled for that day. Stretched in a comfortable chair, I took out my cell phone to call all our family members to give them an update. I understood this particular surgery could take up to twelve hours, so I wandered to a familiar place: the chapel.

After purchasing refreshments to last for the day, I returned to the waiting area as I wanted to stay close by. Hours later, the surgeon appeared and was looking for me. The receptionist pointed him in my direction; with his head bent low he looked very fatigued and stressed out. My anxiety increased to a level that I could hear my heart pounding in my chest. I was frightened by his appearance as he looked so serious and formal.

He sat across from me and, over the sound of my pounding heart, he finally spoke, "The surgery was a success!" The welcome words rang through my heart and soul! They were the words that we had waited so long to hear! I was so relieved that tears of gratitude to God, the surgeon, and all the staff that made this glorious moment possible, coursed down my face in a deluge.

The surgeon continued, "I have to say that he is not *out of the woods* yet. We will take this day to day as he recovers."

I understood that there would be more waiting time with the hope of a healthy recovery. When he finished, I asked, "When can I see him?"

He said, "Very soon."

Before we parted, he prepared me with a warning not to be alarmed at the various racks of medications, life supports, and the ventilator, all of which were necessary for recovery which, little by little, would be removed when the time was right.

I thanked him. Then he explained why he looked so downcast. It had taken all his energy to do this very delicate, intricate surgery of replacing a human organ. Words were not said out loud, but the amount of energy needed in the stress of saving human lives was understood.

Eager to see Tony, I was taken aback as I stood at the doorway. My eyes scanned the room and viewed all the equipment that was keeping my husband alive. I appreciated the surgeon's warning, as this sight would have been overwhelming without it. However, I felt a sense of peace and a ray of hope.

As he lay in recovery, I prayed for strength for him and for all the people who were responsible for this precious gift of life. I prayed for the nurses who would watch over him with twenty-four-hour care during the crucial days ahead. Although he was not awake yet, I was full of hope for a future together once again, side by side, hand in hand; my love for him soared to a new level.

As I sat by his fragile body, I realized he was still fighting for his life and still had a long way to go. I whispered through the taste of salty tears, "I have been a witness to all your struggles, and you are my hero—you made it! It has been my privilege to be your caregiver and especially your wife, during this extraordinary mission, while we waited for the gift of life that you received today."

We thanked God that He had seen fit to restore Tony to me and to our family. Our prayers and those of so many people, family, and friends had been answered. The following Sunday morning my mother attended our church and said the whole congregation stood and cheered when it was announced that the surgery was a success.

While this was our family's journey, we were accompanied by a lot of wonderful people who cared enough to join us on this mission with their love and prayers.

We praise God for His goodness to us and for our *gateway to a new beginning* of a God-centred life together. He was there all the time *while we were waiting*.

Epilogue

Several years have passed since Tony's transplant. We are living our dreams with gratitude and a fresh appreciation for our new life together. Many prayers have been answered and our blessings are too numerous to count.

During his recovery there was still so much to learn, including a new set of instructions in order to keep him healthy. He would have a low immune system for the rest of his life due to the drugs needed to keep his body from rejecting the organ. His special diet and exercise program were important. The new guidelines were similar to what we had been used to, just not quite so strict, which allowed us to go out for dinner and enjoy treats once in a while. It meant a lot to be able to do those things occasionally.

However, since we had been shut in for so long, we were still very cloistered. Instead of feeling like *two birds just let out of a cage* after his surgery, it was quite the opposite. Although the door was open, it took us both a long time to adjust to our new freedom. We were often referred to by our family as hermits; we had somehow forgotten how to branch out into a social setting of any kind.

Although we were elated and grateful for our new start in life, neither of us could explain the pain we were suffering. I called the counselling centre where we had been helped in the past and inquired about this new pain. "Could this sensation be a form of post-traumatic stress disorder?"

The director's answer was clear. "Debbie, people who have suffered much less than this, like even a fall, have suffered from PTSD." I thanked her for her help. There it was—a simple answer that made sense. Yes, that's what it was.

I also shared something else with her that we were both experiencing: the emotional pain of survivor's guilt—the natural reaction of a transplant recipient—while we continued to mourn for the family whose loved one had been the donor. It helped greatly to talk with her. I thanked her for the support she and her staff had been to us while on this journey.

After I hung up, I asked God for more of His comfort and strength to get us both through the next level of healing.

Since the time of the transplant, the YMCA where I worked closed its doors, but God provided another employment opportunity at the very place where we had received so much help and support through the years—South Niagara Life Ministries.

Eventually, we were able to rip off the *band-aid* from our emotional wounds so we could heal, and take a leap of faith, encouraging each other to get out more and do normal things. We went on many picnics, had bike rides along the river, took day trips, and began to accept invitations from family and friends in an effort to regain a social life. As a result, we both continued to heal and life began to feel normal.

A month after Tony's transplant, we were delighted when our first grandson, Calo, was born and three months later our adorable granddaughter, Alanna, arrived. Before long, it was often no longer just the two of us on these outings.

A new confidence set in as we moved forward, grateful for Tony's good health! Just when we thought we were already experiencing *heaven on earth*, we became grandparents to two more precious grandsons, Nathan and Cohen. Many day trips are now spent hand in hand with our grandchildren. We cherish all the special moments of love and joy spent with our children, grandchildren, and even their dogs.

Throughout the entire journey, we had the blessing of a special relationship with God. During most of those years, life was not easy, and we often struggled as each new challenge presented itself. We learned that when we prayed, to ask for help and guidance was important, but the most important part was listening and thanking God for the answers we received. We realized that it was He who led us through every event: the emergencies, the transplant, the recovery, and restored Tony to good health. We thank God for the blessing of His presence *while we were waiting,* and He will continue to be with us as our hope, our strength, and our comforter in all the days to come.

> *"Love is patient and kind. Love is not jealous or boastful or proud or rude. It does not demand its own way. It is not irritable, and it keeps no record of being wronged. It does not rejoice about injustice but rejoices whenever the truth wins out. Love never gives up, never loses faith, is always hopeful, and endures through every circumstance"* 1 Corinthians 13:4-7 (NLT).

To God Be the Glory!

About the Author

For as long as she can remember Debbie has had an interest in writing. As a child, her mother often found her with a pad and pencil in hand. While growing up, her dad was chronically ill.

With the onset of stress and anxiety, she discovered that writing was a way to cope. She often wrote funny stories as a pick-me-up; laughter was an oasis. So, when her husband became chronically ill, it was no surprise she used the pen once again to express her emotions on paper.

With the busyness of life, education, family responsibilities, and many other priorities, she put their story on hold even though she often had a gnawing sensation that God was nudging her to write.

She was inspired when she received a journal titled *When God Smiles at You* from the director at the Centre where she found comfort in counselling as Tony's health continued to decline. It was the title that motivated her to write—about their journey, including spiritual and humorous moments.

Later her sister gave her a second journal, *From the Heart*. As the challenges increased, she wrote about the more serious and emotionally painful times even tear stains grace one page. Writing in both journals created a balance of calamity, courage, caring, and healing with moments of hilarious comedy.

First thing in the morning is her favorite time to read the Bible, enjoy devotional books, and spend time in prayer—just God and her. With God's help, she regained the confidence to continue writing while waiting for her husband's organ transplant.

Many times, she wanted to give up writing, but a dear Christian friend, Irene, encouraged her to continue as she believed the story was special and should be told. This form of therapy brought her closer to God and closer to family and friends. It is her prayer that this story will encourage and inspire others as they walk their own journey of life.

The title *While We Were Waiting* was chosen when she suddenly became the caregiver for her husband. She began writing about their struggles as they went from a comfortable life to the journey of her husband's illness. Writing each chapter with prayer, helped to alleviate the worry and anxiety she felt during times of calamity, caring, compassion, courage, and even a bit of comedy.

Debbie and her husband live in a delightful small town where they often say they feel like they are on vacation. They are blessed to have their son and daughter and their families living nearby. They thank God for His presence as they enjoy life together, hand in hand, side by side.

www.ingramcontent.com/pod-product-compliance
Lightning Source LLC
Chambersburg PA
CBHW030234170426
43201CB00006B/215